10/04

Debt for Sale

Debt for Sale

A Social History of the Credit Trap

BRETT WILLIAMS

PENN

University of Pennsylvania Press

Philadelphia

10   9   8   7   6   5   4   3   2   1

Published by
University of Pennsylvania Press
Philadelphia, Pennsylvania 19104-4011

Library of Congress Cataloging-in-Publication Data
Williams, Brett.
  Debt for sale : a social history of the credit trap / Brett Williams.
     p. cm.
  Includes bibliographical references and index.
  ISBN 0-8122-3817-6 (cloth : alk. paper)—ISBN 0-8122-1886-8 (pbk. : alk. paper)
  1. Consumer credit—United States. 2. Debt—United States. I. Title.

HG3756.U54W534 2004
332.7'43—dc22   2004049453

Contents

Chapter 1
Don't Charge This Book!

After September 11, 2001, ordinary Americans were urged to shop. Patriotic shopping would thwart terrorists, celebrate public life, and pull us back from the abyss of recession. We needed to be good citizen-consumers, but we knew that we could not really save America by shopping. Too many of us already carried too much debt.

In this book, I explore credit and debt in American life. I trace the dizzying change of the last thirty years, when credit upended relations between money, work, time, and property. Debt consumed, even ruined, many Americans. I track the connections between debts and debtors and the lenders and investors who profit from debt. I argue that debt joins rich and poor people all over the world, and I try to illuminate how those connections have been obscured. Debt intensifies class inequalities, but masks them at the same time so that debtors sometimes feel personally responsible for social problems.

Beginning in the 1970s, credit and debt became the engine of the economy. Rampaging through mergers, acquisitions, and leveraged buyouts, corporations piled on debt, moved offshore, laid off workers, and relied more on temporary and part-time help to cut costs and pay back debt. Underemployed workers needed credit to make ends meet. Credit cards acted as welfare or domestic partners for the floundering middle class. The social safety net that government had been providing frayed instead, because government, too, now bore heavy debt from stockpiling arms while granting huge tax breaks to the wealthiest Americans. Wealthy investors grew even wealthier from their returns on the government bonds that serviced government debt.

New computer technologies in the 1970s allowed banks to develop national credit networks of merchants and customers, to gather and process volumes of information on people's lives, to screen users to charge variable interest rates, and to discipline slow payers with penalties and fees. Deregulation in the 1980s allowed many nonbanks to act like banks and issue credit cards too. Powered by profits from interest payments as borrowers sought to repay their debts, banks and faux banks ballooned into megabanks during the next two decades. Some banks faltered from making too many bad loans. Others benefited from friendly regulatory treatment, purchasing portfolios of other banks' debtors or swallowing the other banks whole. In 1972 ten commercial banks in the United States held assets of more than $10 billion. By 1998 only three of those ten banks were still owned by the same companies. In addition, waves of mergers and acquisitions slashed the total number of banks. In 1980 there were fourteen thousand banks, but fewer than ten thousand remained in 1996. Nine thousand issued credit cards, but the top ten controlled 55 percent of the market. The last wave of mergers in 1998 (when, for example, Nations Bank gobbled up Bank of America, along with its name) left many big cities without their own major bank. After 1999 commercial banks could merge with Wall Street investment firms and insurance companies. One side of the firm could consult the other about how to solve its financial difficulties, then both could agree to hide that knowledge from investors. Banks could grow even bigger and monopolize more services. Customers' personal information, including credit reports, banking history, and credit card and Social Security numbers can be shared, traded, and sold down the line. Banks can move assets into affiliates that are not required to comply with the Community Reinvestment Act. The bank side of the firm can consult insurance records in evaluating loans, disguise loans as commodity swaps, or offer insurance and make secret loans to itself.[1]

Lightning-fast communications and computer technologies allow these behemoths to manage massive, far-flung operations with millions of borrowers. Sophisticated equipment and facilities reduce the ultimate costs but require such huge capital investment that only the very biggest banks can participate profitably. Interstate expansion shields them from regional recessions, and ever-bolder combinations of banks, brokerage houses, mortgage lenders, and insurance and mutual fund companies allow them to bridge corporate and consumer finances and make up bad commercial loans with consumer deposits. They subcontract out special detail work such as servicing mortgages, processing credit cards, or haranguing malingerers, and they package portfolios of credit card receivables for sale on capital markets. They also sell bad loans, or charge-offs, to law firms that specialize in taking unlucky debtors to court (rather than simply breaking their kneecaps like the old loan sharks). In the process they compile mountains of personal information on the private details of our lives so that they can customize financial packages for individuals and maximize profits. Banking profits reached an all-time high in 1998 even as banks sold off their loans to Wall Street investors. Financial institutions wield enormous political clout in pursuit of a dangerous agenda, in which local banks and branches disappear to be reborn as fringe banks, and the resulting concentration makes possible escalating fees and interest rates. A banking structure built on debt is bound to be precarious.

The fundamental contradiction in this new system is that consumers must keep the economy growing and the superbanks afloat by taking on debt. The whole point of credit cards, the way they are rendered most profitable, is that we dig ourselves into debt and stay trapped there forever. And it's hard to shop cheerfully or patriotically when we're maxed out. The nasty shadow of the superbank (or is it the other way around?) is the bowed-down-by-debt or bankrupt consumer. The frequent flier who never pays interest for free monthly loans and even makes a profit in rebates and perks, like the deal maker who rides free on the junk-bond-leveraged-buyout express, is buoyed by the usurious interest rates paid by people who borrow to manage emergencies and make ends meet. The reeking underside of the American economy can be measured—not just by fewer, bigger, jury-rigged nonbank superbanks, but by the 1,492,000 bankruptcy filings and the whopping $7.5 trillion owed in consumer debt in 2001. By 2003, our personal debt amounted to 130 percent of our disposable income, up by nearly one-third since 1995.[2]

How did all this come about? Like players in the game of "Risk," bankers moved from state to state, with the credit card their interstate warhorse. They supported and shared research on who could bear debt and just how much could be borne. When the customers who paid their bills promptly turned out to be "deadbeats" by not supporting operations through paying interest, bankers turned to people who were riskier. They sought debtors who would never be able to pay their balance in full, but would faithfully pay interest so that issuers could harvest or sell these mature accounts. Credit card interest and fees were their chief source of profit during the 1980s, propelled by aggressive marketing and sales efforts. They pushed credit cards into pharmacies, grocery stores, and government agencies. Parking tickets, bail bonds, and even income taxes are now debt financed. When the borderline, tenuous, struggling middle class became glutted with debt, bankers moved on to other frontiers: college students, high school students, and the very poor.

Bankers and government economists are not really surprised that we cannot rescue the economy again. They predicted and planned for this saturation of our capacity to borrow and pay back. Financial service executives have lobbied long and hard for their right to offer credit on the most desirable terms for themselves. They fought to preserve the spread between regular interest rates and the sticky interest charged on cards. They wooed legislators through relocating to states like Delaware and South Dakota (which repealed its usury cap altogether). They returned to these lawmakers for favors on such legislation as the new bankruptcy bill in 2002, which allowed only the very wealthy to seek the fresh start that bankruptcy protection provides. They market their product by appealing to our desire to be generous or masterful or mature and play on our need to pay bills, help relatives, or manage emergencies. They have shamelessly seduced college and high school students by appealing to their need for independence, their belief in the value of education, their dreams of success, the illusion that they must build credit histories, and of course their love of parties. Having abandoned retail banking and investment in poor neighborhoods, superbanks have returned there in the guise of grimly plexiglassed storefronts, which offer the most expensive credit of all through payday loans, pawnshops, check-cashing services, and rent-to-own furniture. These usurious lenders further impoverish and disenfranchise people who are already strapped.

We buy things that are already gone by the time we have worked long enough to pay for them. We seem to accept the fact that people who are wealthy are entitled to interest-free loans each month, subsidized by the poorer people who pay high interest rates on their debt. Like the mortgage interest deduction for homeowners, free credit has become a sacrosanct entitlement, while those who pay interest on their credit cards, payday loans, and pawned treasures can no longer deduct that interest from their taxes. In fact, they are likely to pay interest on the money they borrowed to charge their taxes, or to pay especially exorbitant interest if they get a Refund Anticipation Loan by filing their tax return electronically with the tax-processing firm H&R Block.

Some people use credit cards to order concert tickets by telephone, pay for reimbursed travel in advance, keep a record of their income tax deductions, settle large bills a month after purchase so that the money can sit in an interest-bearing account, get free insurance and theft protection, and fly free. Other people pay high interest to maintain a modest standard of living; repair their cars; pay medical bills, utility bills, and tuition; buy durables and groceries; survive widowhood, divorce, and other life transitions; or gamble on enrichment programs like piano and soccer lessons that might give their children a boost to a more secure and abundant life. Many Americans settle for the facades, the illusions, of middle class lives as expensive credit drags us down, and unproductive investment in debt saps the energy of the economy.

We may hate our debt and feel complicit for carrying it, we may be driven crazy trying to elude our creditors, but we have not mobilized our anger at the people and institutions that have choked us with debt. Instead, many of us blame the poor, the welfare state, greedy and impulsive women, or racially marked and foreign others. Despite the many legal instruments that allow the rich to preserve and pass on great fortunes; despite the nearly perfect, cradle-to-grave socialist cocoon of support and protection provided military officers and veterans; and despite handsome mortgage and educational subsidies for the middle class many Americans appear to believe that it is poor people, usually black women, who defy cultural values emphasizing the importance of self-sufficiency and leech off the state. Credit and debt lure and distract us from the real reasons households face economic crisis. We feel grateful that credit cards allow us to go to college or that the pawnbroker financed a prescription or that a payday loan made Christmas possible. People who do not pay interest often confront their "credit others" across a moral divide: other people who pay interest confirm their claims to moral superiority.

Credit is part of the ebb and flow of social life, for nobody is or can be or should be truly self-sufficient. Credit allows people to extend the here and now, to ease transitions, plant crops, go fishing, sell goods in markets, move to a new place, or invest in capital equipment by taking on an obligation to repay the loan during flusher times. Credit can take such simple forms as carpooling or be as complex as the Trobrianders' kula ring, which bound people on dispersed islands in a social web of delayed ceremonial exchanges of arm bands for necklaces.

Credit and debt are also grimly implicated in power relations. People take on debt to large lending institutions in the corporate world. When inequalities between debtors and creditors are too stark, people may enter a modern form of peonage, as they pay for debt by being in hock with their lives, or experience usury when the interest on the debt is so great that it unjustly saps the debtor and perpetuates the inequalities that made it necessary in the first place. Colonial encounters, when indigenous peoples labored to pay for goods they never wanted; sharecropping, when laborers worked to pay for the soil and the seed money that allowed them to plant; human smuggling, which deposits immigrants and sex workers in a new place where they must labor, undocumented, to pay for transport, or structural adjustment programs requiring that developing nations slash social services and domestic industries to secure international loans—all illustrate the unjust power relations and lasting suffering inflicted and buttressed by peonage and usury.

Credit and debt only make sense in the context of other social relations and obligations, and anthropologists have long been interested in the broader context of which debt is a part. Credit is not a gift, but from the creditor's perspective it can act like one. Gifts can be insurance policies or savings accounts, a way to hedge your bets for your own hard times, because gifts often carry with them a statement about a relationship as well as the obligation to give something back.

Credit also implies a relationship of a sort. It can express solidarity and interdependence because you are a member of a gang, a clan, or you are an in-law or *compadre*. Debts may bind you and your group to another group over time as, for example, when Nuer families pay bride wealth cattle to their in-laws for many years to compensate them for the loss of childbearing women. Debt throws you off balance in some way, for there is always a time lag and an asymmetry involved. The crucial questions become Were you dragged into debt or did you ask for credit willingly? When do you have to pay it back, to whom are you indebted, and what sanctions are available to the creditor? Does it lift you up or drag you down, *and is that the essential difference between credit and debt?* Are they the same thing, with the difference in how you experience and perceive it? Are they always double edged, expressing solidarity and separateness, reciprocity and power, promise and threat? Do they go on forever, or do they end, and how do they end if they ever do?

In the United States during the last thirty years, these relations have been so masked that they are almost unrecognizable. We have no cultural language to understand and interpret them, so we often liken credit to freedom and mastery, and debt to addiction, drug abuse, narcissism, low self-esteem, dependency, or a search for immediate gratification. We tend to blame the debtors rather than the institutions that did the irresponsible lending. "Debt porn" fills the pages of popular magazines, where readers can learn about the folly that trapped other people in a downward spiral of debt and memorize the steps that will help them get out. Without debtors' prisons, the end is less sure: we hope for a miraculous change in fortune, the death of a relative, an unusually good year in commissions. Perhaps we'll hit the lottery, find the right consolidation/repayment plan, or file for bankruptcy protection.

There are better metaphors for the relationship between expensive credit and debt: welfare in a lost welfare state or domestic partners in a declining economy where deflated households need more than one worker. The apparently anachronistic concepts of usury and peonage still work too. We live in the most unequal society in the industrialized West. The richest 20 percent of Americans earn nine times more than the poorest 20 percent, and the richest 1 percent of the richest group hold 38 percent of its wealth. Wealthy, powerful institutions extend expensive credit for excessive profits. Credit cards act to obscure, reproduce, and exacerbate divisions of class, race, and gender by creating a credit relationship in which individuals and banks are paired in a patronizing, asymmetrical economy of debt. The illusion of choice and our own feelings of complicity hide the fact that debt is embodied domination, that the purpose of consumer credit is to keep you in debt in perpetuity. You are not supposed to be able to pay enough to escape debt, but you are supposed to pay interest on time or be disciplined by higher interest, penalties, fees, and harping, dunning, threats, and infantilizing phone calls. Your detailed, precise credit history can be stigmatizing or enabling: it is your life, it legitimizes you. Your credit report is accepted as an objective measure of citizenship and personal financial responsibility; it is a seamless, convenient means of reproducing inequality.

In 1976 when my first unsolicited credit card arrived in the mail, and I immediately treated my neighbor and her three sons to dinner at the Cuban restaurant on our block. None of us had any money—she worked as a maid and I was a new assistant professor—and the experience felt magical to us. During the years since, I have marveled that the changes I describe here came so quickly to seem like the natural state of affairs. Despite faithfully reading everything from the *Journal of Retail Banking* to the *Left Business Observer*, despite interviewing dozens of despairing debtors, every financial decision I have made during these years has been a bad one. Trying to cushion the shock of my husband's death, I used credit cards to make sure my children would not be materially deprived on top of their grief. I took on a mortgage I couldn't pay. I bought a nice car and twice pawned it. I took on ill-paying projects to make extra money. Those few friends and relatives I wasn't too ashamed to tell about my struggles bailed me out again and again. I have had judgments brought against me and my salary garnished. I still carry debt, and I will probably always be in debt, although I have not used credit cards in a very long time. I rent a house in a poor neighborhood, and I cannot afford a car. When my sons went to college, despite their mother's experiences, they quickly acquired their own credit cards and maxed them out. I reveal these personal experiences to make very clear the distinction between doing social and economic analysis and living our daily lives. I do not think I am smarter than those of you who may read it. My research has not enabled me to connect the public to the private in a way that might protect my own family from the ravages—the despair, depression, guilt, shame, insomnia, and nightmares—that plague a life in debt. In many ways, I have been an unwilling participant-observer in the social relations I describe. At the same time, my class has protected me. I am a privileged debtor.

Abby Scher writes: "Tell your friends and relatives you're writing an article on credit cards and see what happens. Everybody has a horror story."[3] So true! Because this book is an exposé, I will not make an attempt to be neutral. However, I will try to tell the truth. I have outed myself as a debtor to be clean about my bias, and throughout the book I will rely on full and careful documentation of my claims. Much of my evidence comes from the financial service industry's journals, where they write to each other, sharing information on the world of debtors and strategies for expansion there. I also rely heavily on the writings of economists who are critical of that industry. Other evidence comes from the stories and credit life histories of people who are and are not in debt. Most of this comes from formal interviews. Twice I taught courses on credit and debt, and my students in those courses helped me gather stories, mostly on student debt. Three times my university gave me research grants, and I hired assistants who also interviewed debtors. As I learned from the financial services literature about their widening circles of credit, I began to purposely seek out debtors who were emblematic of the categories of people the industry recognized. I used a kind of snowball sampling, as debtors led me to other debtors who would tell their stories. I also did several formal research projects, during these years, among poor people facing displacement from public housing and seeking work. Their stories invariably concerned debt. I also visited, and borrowed from, fringe banks myself: pawn shops, check-cashing services, and payday loan stores. (I wish I could say this was purely research motivated, but sometimes it was my only option.) I took careful notes and interviewed other customers there. Finally, in addition to all this purposeful methodology, I collected debt porn, almost every day. These stories do more than ornament my argument. They illustrate and flesh out a fundamental point: that we may experience and imagine debt according to different social positions, but that if we listen to each other we can apprehend its whole complexity.

Debt in the United States is fundamentally depoliticized; we all need to connect the dots, see the inequalities and injustices, and cast off our paralyzing feelings of complicity. In addition to following the numbers, I have been helped enormously by reading bankers' own words, and this is why I quote at some length from the different discourses they employ in talking to each other, to us, and to the state. It has helped me to understand how purposeful it has all been, how profitable, and how disingenuous. I see now that bankers should not be surprised that we cannot consume enough to keep the economy afloat. They planned for this to happen all along, but, now that's become a reality, they don't really know how to make it work. The contradictions are too stark.

Although I try to duck the debt collector when she calls my house every day, I also know that MBNA is the prime mover behind the bankruptcy bill that Congress will likely pass. I can almost laugh at my disappointment in Senate cosponsor Tom Daschle, who represents the state that repealed its usury law to lure credit card operations there. Bankruptcy, if not quite a reform of the system, did give debtors a shot at a fresh start. Under the new law, everyone will have to pay more in fees, many will lose their houses and cars, many will not be able to file at all, and many who do file will come out owing exactly the same amount that they filed to escape in the first place. This bill will not affect Chapter 11 filers like Enron and WorldCom, only those people paying usurious interest for groceries, medical care, car repairs, or to survive being laid off from corporations like Enron and World-Com. It will be sent for approval to President Bush, whose top campaign contributor was MBNA.[4]

We debtors need to organize too. We need to insist that being a citizen does not mean being a consumer. We all participate in the same economy. We are all connected to one another. The big borrowers who spent their money on financial services, junk bonds, mergers, takeovers, and leveraged buyouts in a flurry of flexible accumulation also abandoned the productive investment that would have kept our cities livable, our water clean, housing decent, trains running, children vaccinated, education meaningful, and jobs life sustaining. This book is about the connections between credit and debt, power and inequality, the Ponzi schemes in the boardroom and the power tool in the pawnshop.

Chapter 2

Calling All Convenience Users

Credit cards have transformed the relationships between our time, our work, our possessions, and our money. In this chapter I explore the extraordinary innovations that made credit cards possible. Some of these innovations involved expensive computer systems, whose downside was that only the biggest banks could afford to revamp them every few years and before long these corporate giants were peering into our private lives. I examine government's tentative pokes at regulating the challenges posed by credit card technology: telling customers the truth about debt, ensuring their privacy, and preventing fraud. Government poked even more tentatively at issues of equal access to debt and the disastrous potential of unrestrained debt. I also introduce the first of several credit life stories, through the experiences and perspectives of an early card user. Sought out by bankers, she foiled them, because she brought to credit cards a set of sound banking principles from an earlier era. Bankers mistakenly assumed that people like her would be valuable credit card customers, and when they weren't, faced a quandary about how to use borrowers to turn a profit. Credit cards generate many inequalities, and one inequality was revealed early on through the enthusiastic responses of convenience users to free credit and the perks they gained along with it. I place these developments in the larger cultural context of the 1970s, for this was an important transitional time when the opportunity to build a road to a more just society was lost, and credit was a major dynamic in this detour.

Americans have long relied on credit and debt to outlast hard times. Some Americans borrowed by "book credit" at the grocery store as early as during the Revolutionary War.[1] With the growth of assembly lines, mass production, and advertising in the early twentieth century, buying large durable goods on time became customary, with poor people buying the used cars created by planned obsolescence.[2] Total debt outstanding doubled in each of the first two decades of the twentieth century, then doubled again in the 1920s, and again between 1933 and 1939. Before World War I, Americans borrowed through banks and small loan institutes or bought in installments from the makers or sellers of such durables as pianos and sewing machines. Poorer people who could not get loans this way paid usurious, illegal interest to loan sharks and pawnbrokers.[3] For many poor people, debt was a way of life. It was especially onerous for African American sharecroppers in the South, who were tied to the land by the debts they owed to landowners after borrowing seeds, fertilizer, and food between harvests. The debt peonage of the poor was sometimes enforced by the violent repayment practices of urban loan sharks or by lynching and rape in the South.[4]

Middle- and upper-class Americans have known and used paper and metal charge cards since the early twentieth century in such places as department stores and gasoline stations. These cards were not meant to be profitable by themselves, but they helped businesses expand their customer base and boost big-ticket items. Mom-and-pop stores also offered credit to loyal customers through such informal means as "running a tab" and putting purchases on layaway. After World War II, the growth of suburbs, shopping malls, and corporate retail chains brought ruin to many of these smaller stores. White middle-class Americans formed new nuclear family households in record numbers and filled their starved homes with the furniture and appliances they had felt deprived of during the Depression and the war. They, and their banks, grew ever more interested in credit. Small consumer loans allowed them to buy sofas, refrigerators, and pianos. Car loans were especially attractive to banks, for cars provided solid collateral for longer loans. Cars became essential to the new, more mobile American lifestyle, gas essential to cars, and credit essential to both.

But these small consumer loans were costly to banks. Without computerized accounting technologies, bank loan officers had to approve each installment loan application, regardless of amount. Subsequent loan payments required laborious and expensive documentation. Bankers speculated that Americans might opt for the convenience and prestige of an all-purpose credit card. Why should people carry different loans for cars, refrigerators, sofas, sewing machines, and pianos when they could owe all their money to one source? Why not offer an all-encompassing card to replace customers' myriad debt relationships with small stores? Why not bind them more completely and complexly to the bank? Thus the idea of relationship banking—consolidating a number of personal financial functions with one institution—was born.

This was first a period of exuberant growth and then monumental concentration. Department stores and oil companies had offered credit operations at a small loss. But credit became for banks an end in itself. They planned to realize profits by providing paying customers to businesses and offering these customers quick, convenient access to goods and services.

Lenders' profits would come from a percentage of business income and, they hoped, from the interest paid by credit card holders over time.

Bankers built on the experiences of department stores with such practices as a grace period between purchase and payment. They also built on their own early experiments in the business charge market pioneered by such credit-granting pioneers as Diners Club, Carte Blanche, and American Express in the 1950s. These accounts offered business travelers a national network of travel and entertainment venues, but borrowers had to pay their monthly balances in full.

By the summer of 1958, a mass marketing campaign was primed for the BankAmericard. It began with the first mass mailing of more than sixty thousand unsolicited credit cards to existing Bank of America customers in Fresno, California. Over the next twelve years, nearly one hundred million unsolicited credit cards flooded U.S. households. These drops netted many free riders and also unscreened users such as children, dogs, and dead people; they provoked citizen outrage when the cards were intercepted and used illegally. Banks speculated wildly about who was committing this fraud. Some argued that prostitutes were the biggest perpetrators (for they lifted them from men's wallets) or that merchants copied charge slips to counterfeit cards. Others imagined that prisoners or other low-life crooks ran cottage industries based on buying and fencing, shaving and pasting, flat ironing and reembossing blank cards with valid names and account numbers. In Chicago, where postal clerks were accused of intercepting unmailed credit cards so that they could sell them on the black market, the Mafia was implicated.[5]

New regional bank systems facilitated the rapid expansion of consumer and merchant networks across state boundaries. Together with the resulting economies of scale (power through largeness), these regional systems laid the foundation for a national infrastructure for marketing credit cards, processing transactions, and reducing fraud. By 1970, Master Charge had expanded into forty-nine states, while BankAmericard operated in forty-four states.[6]

However, this precomputerized world was littered with unwieldy pieces of paper. Bankers needed to make speedy decisions about approving unsolicited cards, but to do so they had to check a printed "hot list" of delinquent users which could never be kept current. Or they had to telephone. Joseph Nocera writes:

Then there was the business of authorization, which went hand in hand with interchange . . . the merchant had to call his bank, and while he was put on hold, his bank would make a long distance call to the bank that had issued the credit card, and while *it* was put on hold, the clerk on the other end of the line would pull out a fat printout of names and numbers and look up the customer's balance to see if the purchase could be approved—all while the customer and the merchant stood in the store, waiting for the reply. And that was when the system was operating *smoothly*. Sometimes the merchant got a busy signal. Other times his call went unanswered, something that happened most often when a customer with a card from an East Coast bank tried to buy something late in the day in California. And if he couldn't get through, the merchant then had to decide whether to accept the card or lose the sale. And if he took the card, and it turned out to be stolen, all hell would break loose as the banks fought over who should absorb the loss.[7]

Banks also wanted to transfer sales information faster to speed billing, but they had to mail charge slips around the country, from merchants to customers, to make sure they were correct. As the scope of credit card operations grew national and the volume of transactions multiplied, the credit card industry centralized their processing operations through computerized switching systems. These on-line systems facilitated direct-mail solicitations, helped banks expand their reach, and allowed them to refine relationship banking by linking credit lines to checking accounts or other loans.[8]

In 1976, BankAmericard changed its name to Visa to foster a more international and cosmopolitan image, and Master Charge changed its name to MasterCard (perhaps to mask the reality of the transaction). Although some banks tried to remain independent, most joined in this trend. By 1978, more than eleven thousand banks had abandoned their own operations and had affiliated with either Visa or MasterCard or both. By the end of the decade more than half of the cards were issued by only fifty banks, including such major players as Citibank, Bank of America, First National, Chase Manhattan, and the Bank of Chicago. In 1977, Citicorp's mass mailing of Visa applications yielded three million new accounts, and Citicorp became the leading issuer of bank credit cards.[9]

While credit cards quickly came to seem like a natural, permanent feature of American life, they actually proliferated as a response to a banking challenge in the 1970s. Responding to harsh American policies in the Middle East, in 1974 the oil-producing nations (OPEC) began to withhold the oil on which we were too dependent. Crude oil prices increased 500 percent in seven years. Oil shortages drove up the cost of gasoline and almost everything else. (While some people saw the problem of oil prices as a cultural crisis that challenged our overreliance on automobiles and overconsumption of gasoline, policy makers treated the problem as a shortage of supply that demanded more political and military control over the rebellious Arab states.)[10] In addition, food harvests failed around the world, pushing up prices for food. Prices escalated during the decade, and nobody seemed to know how to manage this frightening inflation. The oil-producing nations deposited their profits in American banks, because American dollars were all over the world.[11] Banks at first invested this money by making loans to countries that were struggling with development in the face of inflation and by bankrolling the suburban developments that were erupting into the American countryside. They misjudged badly: countries struggling with inflation couldn't pay off these loans, and developers overbuilt the suburbs, creating monstrous, empty developments in many parts of the country. Their other source of profits—home mortgages—were compromised in two ways. People who had bought houses in the 1950s and 1960s were riding their debt on inflation and in effect paying the banks with devalued dollars. As inflation depleted the value of dollars, it almost appeared as if the mortgage debt paid itself.[12] In addition, the stagnant economy made it hard for other people to take on mortgages at all. Thus, investing in credit cards proved to be a brilliant maneuver that saved banks and ultimately brought huge profits to the few that could afford the costly technology.

Struggling for Equal Access: What Should *Congress* Do?

In the 1970s wrenching change was taking place. The Vietnam War ended, and the Civil Rights movement had inspired many activists to claim rights and opportunities of their own. Civil rights pressures even buoyed the Free DC movement, and the District of Columbia at last won limited home rule. The government in turn was supposed to safeguard those rights through offices and procedures accessible to ordinary citizens. For example, in 1972 the federal Department of Health, Education, and Welfare threatened to pull federal contracts from universities, even the most elite and prestigious ones, because they refused to address their failure to hire and promote women faculty.[13] However, these changes holding that all Americans were equal citizens were very new and still contested, creating the strange climate surrounding the passage of the Equal Credit Opportunity Act.

This landmark legal battle asked a fundamental question about credit: Was it a civil right? In 1974 not everybody believed that women had the right to hold credit on their own. What about a *company's* right to determine creditworthiness? Should banks be forced to take risks on just anyone?

A diverse coalition of women's groups organized for passage of the Equal Credit Opportunity Act. Women's groups documented persuasively that single women had more trouble gaining credit than single men did and that once a woman married she had to reapply for credit in her husband's name. Married women could not get credit in their own names, nor could they count their income when the couple applied for credit. Once a woman was divorced or widowed she had great difficulty being deemed "creditworthy." "Hormones, birth control and wedding rings are not matters of credit," argued Betty Furness before the Subcommittee on Consumer Affairs of the Committee on Banking and Currency.

The successful passage of the Equal Credit Opportunity Act promised nondiscrimination on the basis of sex, marital status, race, color, religion, national origin, or age. However, most of the details were hammered out later when the Federal Reserve Board, under heavy lobbying from citizens and bankers, patched together the regulations that would mandate the terms for credit access. Bankers argued that the elementary telephone and paper technology of credit card operations required that their credit investigations be cheap and efficient. They told the Federal Reserve Board that those individual qualities that seemed to be sexist also held enormous predictive power. They *needed* to consider whether or not a woman had changed her name when she married because that was evidence of how long the marriage might last. And they disagreed with Betty Furness about birth control. What if a woman was not using contraception? Didn't a company need to know if she were on the verge of becoming pregnant and thus less creditworthy? Didn't pregnancy mean that she might give birth, increase her financial liabilities, and lose her job? And weren't age and race important determinants of an applicant's continuing ability to pay? Bankers' curiously Victorian questions about how to appraise potential customers certainly showed them to be a few steps behind the feminist movement. The Federal Reserve Board stood firm against many of the industry's minor, administrative challenges to women's rights, but it allowed bankers to take age into account if the criteria were standardized and effective. The board also allowed banks to surreptitiously continue to score race, class, and national origin, using zip codes as their proxy. If you lived, for example, in an African American, Haitian, Ethiopian, Colombian, or Cambodian neighborhood, or were a resident of an identifiably hard-knocks area, your zip code could taint your score. Ultimately, gaining equal access to credit was a partial victory.[14]

Ironically, the equal access issues that had been so contested ended up moot with the advent of increasingly complex rating systems. Banks began to develop the computer technologies that would enable them to discriminate through increasingly individualized quantitative scores. These were based on a large spectrum of criteria ranging from money management to hobbies and personal tastes. These technologies were so expensive that only the giant institutions survived. By 1991 one credit card processing company had developed forty-eight different characteristics for measuring a credit card holder, including how frequently the person used the card, how promptly that person paid, and how often for the full amount. Some industry analysts called this "psychographics" and used the new science to help sell their lists for special advertising. They could also use psychographics to monitor people who did pay in full every month to see if they might soon be in trouble. "Generic data" like demographics is not nearly as useful—and can raise discrimination questions, argued one banker. By contrast, the computer could make sense of myriad pieces of information very quickly and cheaply. In just a few years, computers could assign such precise behavior scores to people that lenders could allegedly predict whether a newly delinquent account would default or not, helping them decide whether to mount a prompt collection effort, step in and cut credit off entirely, or grant the troubled cardholder an increase in credit to help with hard times. Citicorp collected purchasing data on 2 million shoppers at supermarket chains around the country, assembled individualized bundles of coupons for households, and then further refined this data when some people responded. The TRW credit bureau claimed to be able to organize all 150 million Americans into matrices of 600 different categories—ranging from age to whether or not you were a fishing enthusiast.[15] By 1991 Capital One had developed software that allowed the company to issue credit cards precisely tailored to each person's unique buying habits and personal foibles. By 2003, as we will see, your credit score could mean more in any transaction than your salary or personal qualities: from renting an apartment, buying a car, getting a job, to keeping a spot in public housing. Fine-tuned, individual profiles eliminated the lenders' need for generalizations, but it gave the credit score an immense amount of power. Equal access was purely a formality.

The struggle over the Equal Credit Opportunity Act illuminates many of the watershed qualities of the 1970s as well as the ways in which the expansion of credit cards reflected and changed the course of history. Since the passage of the Civil Rights Act in 1964 and the establishment of the Equal Employment Opportunity Commission in 1965, the government had received and responded to many complaints about racial and gender discrimination. Even women's groups still struggled with different ideas about women's rights as full citizens: Should women be treated as special in some ways because of their unique family roles as wives and mothers dependent upon a male breadwinner to at least help support them and their children? Or should they be treated legally as equal to men? Could legislation that protected women on the job as a special class of people also be turned against them? Should feminists focus their efforts on fighting for access to traditionally male-dominated occupations such as university professorships, or should they organize for better pay as household workers, secretaries, and flight attendants? When women did gain access to men's occupations, did that occupation simply lose value?[16]

Welfare rights activists had fought hard for the poverty programs of the

1960s, which had brought some, but never enough, economic support to poor families. Should middle-class, heterosexual women make common cause with poor women, and with people who belonged to sexual minorities? Was inequality a feminist issue? Was a guaranteed income a civil right? The right to a legal abortion had only recently been safeguarded in the Supreme Court case of Roe vs. Wade in 1973, which was a huge victory for women's reproductive rights. But policy makers were still uncomfortable with single mothers and continued to debate what to do with them if they were poor. Would good jobs lift single mothers out of poverty? Or should public programs focus on empowering men and encouraging marriage?[17]

These are familiar questions today, but to many people in the 1970s they seemed new and revolutionary. The issues they addressed were hidden by what seemed to be a great victory: ensuring that middle-class women could qualify for credit just as men could, without their gender, marital status, or birth control practices being scored.

The larger economic problems were certainly masked by the expansion of credit. In addition to the painful inflation that seemed to suck up wages, the economy seemed stagnant. Factories closed to move to places where workers were desperate, labor was cheap, and unions were weak. Business profits grew as the federal deficit soared, and businesses and banks failed to invest money in factories, productive equipment, or residential construction, which would have provided jobs. Rather, they invested in consumer and government debt, which perpetuated the stagnation. Because they did not use their profits in productive ways, unemployment grew because there were few jobs for people entering or displaced from the labor force. Wages fell, and many people were dragged into jobs to help their families make ends meet.[18] Young men could work in the new all-volunteer army established by Nixon. They were disproportionately poor and black, because black unemployment had skyrocketed.[19] Many households needed more than one income, so women who might in earlier times have stayed home to raise children went to work outside. As more and more couples divorced, women were especially pressed to work outside the home, suffering loss of income and decline of standard of living.

Struggling over Interest Rates: What Did the *Supreme Court* Do?

Until the end of the nineteenth century, the United States enforced strict antiusury laws, which capped the annual interest rate on personal loans at 6 percent.[20] Only the poor who were forced into quasi-legal loans had to pay higher rates. These laws reflected an old Jeffersonian belief (perhaps presaged by both the Bible and the Koran) that wealth should come through work, not money lending.

In 1978 the regulation of interest rates posed a political headache for bankers, because many state legislatures still had strict usury laws, which limited the interest rates banks could charge on their credit cards. These laws thwarted banks seeking customers and profits nationwide, because so many states protected their citizens from usury. Many states had passed these plucky laws upon gaining statehood, as among their very first laws, to demonstrate their opposition to loaning money at excessive interest rates. Usury ceilings varied enormously, from 12 percent in Minnesota to 24 percent in the District of Columbia. Many bankers believed that these usury laws posed unreasonable restrictions on the flow of credit. They saw it as price control and argued that competition, not price control, was a better tool for regulating interest.[21]

In 1978 the First National Bank of Omaha won a unanimous, little-noted Supreme Court decision, which liberated credit card operations from elected officials' standards of fair interest. The case began when Marquette National Bank of Minneapolis enrolled in the BankAmericard plan and brought suit against a MasterCard bank, First National Bank of Omaha. Marquette argued that Omaha should not solicit customers in Minnesota until it complied with *Minnesota* usury laws, which set interest rates at 12 percent. Omaha argued that these price controls did more harm than good, because many consumers did not have the credit score to justify a loan at a low rate and that it should be allowed to charge *Nebraska's* rates of 18 percent. The working class and poor people of Minnesota, Omaha declared, would benefit from their services. The court ruled that federal law allows a national bank to charge interest on any loan at the rate allowed by the laws of the state in which the bank is located. Therefore, the court saw the question as one of where the Omaha Bank was "located," in this case, Nebraska.

But Marquette contested this decision, proposing that a bank was not simply bricks and mortar, but in effect a set of transactions as it solicited customers and collected money. Thus it was no more located in Nebraska than in Minnesota. Furthermore, if predatory big banks could export their home interest rates wherever they liked, they would sidestep state legislatures who, Marquette argued, had set current, democratic, fair usury ceilings. Although the Supreme Court decision bears Marquette's name, Marquette lost the fight.[22]

With Omaha's victory in the Supreme Court, several national banks began to market their cards aggressively across the entire country, acquiring the operations of those banks strapped for cash or unable to compete effectively. Citibank, for example, hailed its credit card as its "interstate warhorse," the key to building a nationwide retail market in advance of anticipated legislation making full-scale interstate branching possible. By

1980, Citibank had persuaded South Dakota to be the first state to repeal its anti-usury law, and Citibank rewarded South Dakota by relocating its credit-card processing operations there to become one of the state's largest employers.

Thus the Marquette decision led to more concentration in the industry, as national banks roared across state lines and gobbled up smaller banks. This process has escalated during the last twenty-five years, and we have all seen the fruits of Marquette in our cities. Until 1994, bank holding companies had to set up separately capitalized and managed banks in each state where they did business. But in 1994 the Riegle-Neal Interstate Banking and Branching Bill zoomed through Congress. This law allows banks to consolidate sub-sidiary banks into *branches* of a single bank, thus streamlining operations and reducing overhead. It allows for the creation of behemoths. As just one ex-ample from 2003, the BB & T Corporation, headquartered in Winston-Salem, North Carolina, is a fast-growing, highly profitable financial holding company with $79.6 billion in assets. Its bank subsidiaries operate more than 1,100 branch offices in the Carolinas, Virginia, West Virginia, Kentucky, Georgia, Maryland, Tennessee, Alabama, Indiana, Florida, and Washington, D.C. BB & T ranks number 1 in market share in West Virginia, number 2 in North Carolina, number 3 in Kentucky and South Carolina, number 4 in Virginia, number 5 in Washington, number 6 in Georgia, and number 7 in Maryland. With the Marquette decision and the Riegle-Neal law, state usury laws have become virtually redundant.[23]

Struggling over Credit: What Could *President Carter* Have Done?

We know Jimmy Carter today as a courageous, generous ex-president. He and Rosalyn Carter have spoken out and worked hard for human rights, for peace, and for a shared commitment to affordable housing through Habi-tat for Humanity. His presidency is more troubling. The humbling of the Republican Party after Watergate and the end of the disastrous war in Viet-nam gave Carter a wonderful, rare opportunity to build on the civil rights activism and progressive antipoverty legislation of the 1960s. During his presidency, optimistic antiwar, feminist, black, Latino, environmental, fired-up post-Stonewall gay rights and fired-up post-Alcatraz American Indian activists provided the popular support for the progressive causes that liber-als in Congress might enact.[24] Some activists pulled together and founded Common Cause. The civil rights movement had dramatically affected Carter himself, and in his election he won 90 percent of African American votes. Carter's unpretentious style was expressed by his democratic, inclu-sive inauguration, in which he walked the mile and a half to the White

House and invited campaign volunteers to informal parties held throughout the city of Washington.

However, Carter was stymied by inflation, an organized and cohesive business lobby, and his own timidity about embracing big, good government.[25] This timidity perhaps stemmed from his Depression childhood and his farmer father's fury at President Roosevelt's Agricultural Adjustment Administration, which Carter experienced as "the slaughter of the little pigs and the plowing up of cotton."[26]

Carter spearheaded a few progressive initiatives in unemployment, most notably the 1977 Program for Better Jobs and Income, which raised the minimum wage. Jimmy Carter's approach to the "drug problem" was to decriminalize drug abuse. He strongly backed attempts to legalize marijuana, for example. He doubled the area of the national parks and wildlife refuges, approved the Superfund to clean up toxic waste, and established the Department of Education.[27] He appointed more blacks and women than his predecessors put together, especially to judgeships. But primarily President Carter repudiated the Roosevelt heritage of big government. He did not approve of large-scale government spending, and he hoped to decentralize power and rely on private responsibility. His priorities appeared to be military spending and fighting inflation rather than social programs, disappointing many of his black supporters. He wanted to trim social security benefits and cut back on urban, health, and welfare programs. He persuaded Congress to deregulate transportation, laying the way for the thoroughly deregulated Reagan Revolution in the debt-riddled 1980s.[28]

Then, in his last year in office, in March 1980, President Carter shocked the retail banking industry by abruptly, courageously triggering the Credit Control Act of 1969. This measure ordered banks holding more than $2 million in outstanding consumer credit to establish special deposits with the Federal Reserve Bank. Banks were required to deposit 15 percent of the new credit they extended from then on, on which they would not earn any interest. Carter and the Federal Reserve Board thus imposed a penalty on those banks that continued to expand outstanding consumer credit.

The order held out crucial exceptions: for mortgages, home improvement, home equity, utility, small business, farm, auto, and student loans. President Carter's intent was clear: he wanted to squeeze credit card operations, to decrease the flow of money, and restore the value of the dollar. Carter argued that restraining credit would encourage savings and that money would then be channeled to productive investment in order to increase the supply of goods. But consumer demand for those goods would be slack, because customers' access to credit would be limited. Thus credit restraint would dampen inflation in two ways: by encouraging saving rather than borrowing and by increasing the supply of goods over the demand for them. The industry was outraged. The newly established *Journal of Retail Banking* railed: "It is unlikely that anyone of the FRB actually believes this."

The rule, argued bankers, created a dizzying maze of oppressive regulations and the constraints brought with them extra burdensome costs. The most appropriate analogy, they claimed, lay in the costs involved in requiring mass transit to offer access to the "handicapped." Expensive "retro-fitting" ultimately undermined the nation's real goal of achieving inexpensive mass transit, because the cost to riders was increased in order to subsidize that retrofitting. Just as they had argued in the fight over usury, bankers argued disingenuously that the Credit Controls Act would hurt the people who were most vulnerable. The squeeze on credit cards, they claimed, would benefit the big retail storeowners who could afford their own cards. These large stores would gain business lost by small stores that relied on bankcards, which would now be limited.

The industry also insisted that the regulation would harm people of limited means, including those just establishing credit histories, women, minorities, and the elderly, for they had less flexibility and fewer alternatives to bank credit cards. Banks would have no choice but to raise the cutoff score in their credit scoring system as they struggled to determine who their really important customers were. They could no longer use "human judgment" to override such quantitative features as the employment standard, and sticking to that standard would hurt divorced and widowed women just entering the job market. Finally, the new service fees that they would be forced to charge would ensnare the poor and cultivate a new form of debt peonage, because, like sharecroppers before them, poor people would never be able to pay off their debt.[29]

President Carter abruptly terminated the program just six months later, in July. However, banks seized this opportunity to implement costlier credit for good. They tightened their credit scoring criteria, reduced new credit lines, hoisted rates, and changed the terms of payment, by, for example, raising the monthly minimum. Between 1979 and 1981 they still lost lots of money. For example, Citibank lost over $500 million on credit card operations.[30] In 1981, a pivotal year, they started charging customers annual fees.

The quality of life in the 1980s might have been different if the Federal Reserve Board had more decisively restrained consumer credit in 1980. Amidst all the turmoil of new credit card operations and the extraordinary changes they wrought in American social relations, the government remained inert with uncertainty, making the industry's outrage and resistance to any sort of regulation remarkable and effective. Credit cards in fact were monumentally *un*regulated, as witnessed by the weak Equal Credit Opportunity Act, which slipped in zip codes, the Marquette decision, which allowed banks to transport high interest rates wherever they liked, and the short life of Carter's brave credit controls program.

Rather than try to harness debt, the federal government stuck to the relatively piddling matters of fraud, privacy, and full disclosure. As examples, the Federal Privacy Act aimed to protect customers from unauthorized use of their cards and to forbid companies to rent out their lists of customers. The Fair Credit Billing Act gave customers sixty days to make written complaints. When this law was revised, customers won the right to return shoddy merchandise. It also required companies to provide a written statement of these rights once a year. It prompted Rene Ramirez to write an amusing article on how to make these statements more comprehensible. She suggested using plain English and limiting sentences to fifteen words. But she acknowledged that to do so would be difficult "because so many compound and subjunctive clauses were necessary." Despite her efforts, we have this law to thank for the dense, confusing, microscopic jargon on the back of our credit card statements.

Similarly, the Truth in Lending Act requires creditors to disclose the costs and terms of credit *before* customers take on debt. This act also gives customers the right to cancel certain transactions and mandates that creditors maintain procedures for handling complaints. The Electronic Funds Transfer Act requires banks to disclose terms and conditions before the first electronic transfer is made. It also limits liability for unauthorized use, outlaws unsolicited cards, limits liability for unauthorized use, and requires banks to maintain procedures for handling errors.[31]

These small efforts to protect our privacy have not worked. By 1991 many creditors could know how many times you go out to eat, what kind of food your dog likes, and how likely you are to buy cigarettes or to pay your Visa bill on time. The credit agency Equifax began to produce compact disks filled with our creditworthiness, criminal records, and driving history, marrying the personal computer with the mammoth databases of credit bureaus. By 1996 *Consumer Reports* warned, they "can pull information from many different sources . . . providing [the card company] whatever you need to form a complete picture of your customer, including purchases and payments, response to promotions, and usage patterns, combined with overlays of demographic, census, and lifestyle data." Card issuers can find out your household income, where you shop, what you buy, your age, number of children, your sports and leisure activities, where you like to travel, the magazines you read, even the type of birth-control device you use. These violations of your privacy do not even ensure you of an accurate credit report. If a creditor makes a mistake, your ex-spouse has a problem, or somebody else has your name, your credit report may be tarnished without your knowledge.[32]

And as for fraud: by 2002 cyberbazaars thrived on the Internet, offering credit card numbers in bulk at about $100 for 240 cards. Relying on the efforts and skills of "black-hat hackers" who broke into online merchants' computer systems, these thieves fenced the cards, made purchases, and got cash advances. More routinely, customers may find that illegitimate withdrawals have been made from ATMs in their name, and they are responsible for proving that fraud has occurred.[33]

Only the Community Reinvestment Act of 1977, mandating responsible lending in communities where banks were located, looked seriously at how banks should use money. Consider the implications of this law, passed at the dawn of the credit card era: Federally regulated financial institutions "have a continuing and affirmative obligation to help meet the credit needs of the local communities in which they are chartered."

Banks must identify the credit needs of their communities, and they must demonstrate that they are helping to meet those needs. One year before the Marquette case, Congress had assumed that a bank was part of a community and bore the obligation to behave responsibly there. The act seeks to redress the financial desolation wrought by banks' abandonment of poor urban and rural communities. It has rarely been enforced, and one-time House of Representatives Speaker Newt Gingrich termed it "the worst law of all time." It testifies to a nearly forgotten conviction about money, social responsibility, and the public good.[34]

When we look at the past, we often do so through foggy, selective memory. Using different lenses brings certain qualities of the past into sharper focus. One could look back to the 1970s and see the Community Reinvestment Act, which fortified and expanded the purview of the Home Mortgage Disclosure Act (1975), as part of a tapestry of laws that built on the legacy of civil rights activism in being generous, optimistic, and sometimes weakly enforced. As examples, the Alaska Native Claims Settlement Act (1971), Indian Health Care Improvement Act (1974), Indian Education Act (1972), and Indian Self-Determination and Education Assistance Act (1975)[35] expanded many civil rights protections to include and assist native peoples. The Archaeological Resources Protection Act (1979) aimed to protect the heritage of the past. The Clean Air and Clean Water Acts focused on protecting the environment, and the Comprehensive Employment and Training Act (1973), which created sustainable, skills-building jobs for impoverished people, often in community-based organizations. The National Consumer Cooperative Bank Act (1978) aimed to set aside funds for low-interest loans to start cooperatives.[36] The Equal Credit Opportunity Act, despite its flaws, reads like a mission statement for diversity and inclusiveness today. We have not seen such a burst of progressive legislation since.

There are many other lenses for examining this time period. Music lovers may remember Marvin Gaye's "What's Going On" from 1971, which launched a decade buoyed by the exuberance of funk—Isaac Hayes, the Isley Brothers, James Brown. Funk is dear to many Washingtonians, who also remember the coming of Home Rule, CETA jobs, the birth of funk's child go-go, the opening of the Anacostia Neighborhood Museum, and Summer in the Parks. Other hometowns hold other special memories. The Stonewall rebellion helped launch a new awareness of the oppression of lesbians and gay men, and the decade was marked by gay rights activism. The world celebrated its first Earth Day in 1970, and some would argue that the environmental movement is the struggling progressive movement's most lasting legacy. Others might say it was the Bicentennial Celebration, which refused to honor Columbus, the United Migrant Farmworkers' persistent boycott of iceberg lettuce, or a revival of organic foods and the importance of a healthy, strenuous life. Others see the rebirth of the New Right, which simmered along after Watergate, lashing back at these new forces and bringing new issues such as crime to national attention. America's great military buildup began in 1978, the last year that black income increased relative to whites. Credit cards can also act as a lens, offering a bird's eye view of the 1970s, for they highlight the emotional tug of war between progressive, liberal reform and unfettered capitalism. The winner, it turns out, was the latter, as credit cards helped to drive American society to an increasingly unequal and authoritarian state. I turn now to the experiences and views expressed by Madeline Smith, who exemplifies to me the promise and pitfall of credit cards during this time.

A Model Customer? The Hurdle of the Convenience User

I talked to her often before our formal interview in 1997. We met in an Indian restaurant in upper Northwest Washington, where she has lived for more than thirty years. Graced by a long Indonesian skirt purchased in the Netherlands, she looked fit and much younger than her seventy years, a tribute to her spirited and careful living.

With unmarred credit, a working husband, a house, a savings account, and a steady job, Madeline Smith promised to be an ideal credit card holder. The problem was that she brought her old-fashioned banking ethos to a brave new world in which dizzy consumption and out-of-control debt were the order of the day. Ultimately, she, and others like her, foiled bankers and forced them to search for people who were less creditworthy. In this section, I explore her experiences with and perceptions of credit cards, their proper use and abuse, and examine her outlook on the people who use them differently than she does.

Madeline Smith is a government worker married to a retired economist. She has three grown children, all in business and dispersed around the country. She has thriving grandchildren and a failing stepmother-in-law who now preoccupy her attention.

Smith grew up during the Depression. It marked her. She explains her perspective on money: "Older Americans were brought up to believe that no matter how much you have, you can use it for other purposes; don't pay interest, don't waste your money. No matter how rich you are you still have patterns. Some just have character, a different attitude; maybe it's genetic."

She remembers the years when her children were young, and the family moved into the heart of a blossoming retail area. It was 1959: Woodward and Lothrop had just opened an uptown department store, and so had Saks Fifth Avenue. "I remember saying, 'Well you can't have that' . . . we couldn't buy things." Although she had never intended to, she went to work for the government when her children were quite small, because "we didn't have enough money," expanding her family's income just as many other women did in the postwar period. "We did use cards for school clothes, at Woodies and Sears." However, she has always used credit cards carefully and conservatively, especially for shopping: "I don't know how much I spend . . . maybe $500 a month, except to buy large quantities of wine, maybe then $1,500.00. [Her husband and she are gourmet cooks and wine aficionados.] I don't buy that much. I'm always careful not to overspend . . . it's easier. Anyway, "just write a check," they say, all over the world, even in Hong Kong, if you're foreign and a certain age."

Smith sticks mostly to one Visa card, because it carries no annual fee. She is not sure which bank holds her Visa—perhaps Virginia Citibank. It doesn't really matter, because she pays no interest and feels no special relationship with her bank. She receives many other offers in the mail, but doesn't look at them seriously. "Interest rates are not a consideration. It's the no annual fee and what you get." Alert to new possibilities, she has considered switching to a Visa that offers a 1 percent discount on all purchases. Smith takes pride in the values that have influenced her use of credit, and she believes that this sense of responsibility can be taught:

Credit cards facilitate trade and economics, but some people just don't know how to handle it, like alcohol. There's a built-in corrective: abuse it and lose it is the best discipline. If you don't know how to drive a car, you can lose your license. We shouldn't have to take care of adults.

Children should be made to understand what it represents . . . just like cigarette advertising. You have to be knowledgeable and not believe everything everybody tells you. Explain things to children so they understand.

She is proud that her own kids "don't borrow, don't buy, don't have . . ." But when her children have needed money, for example to buy a house, she writes a check against her securities: "They charge the prime—7–8 percent—and we charge [them] what we pay." Smith thus offers her children a highly discounted loan at an interest rate much lower than the 19–20 percent rates that they would probably pay if they used credit cards. Their access to inexpensive credit also provides a certain personal power and credibility. Yet her class-based access to inexpensive credit appears to her to be a matter of her family's values rather than a product of class privilege. Smith believes that credit cards represent progress, and that is emphatically a good thing; technological advances have allowed sure authorizations and quick checkouts, and carrying credit cards has probably meant that there are fewer robbers:

They've made it easier, like to go shopping. Before if you didn't take your checkbook, and you saw things you wanted you couldn't buy them. But they haven't changed my standard of living at all.

The more uses the better! You shouldn't go back on economic development. They're good for the economy; people spend and that is good [for] economic growth, don't go back to the old ways of saving money under the mattress. People didn't live as well. I think they're great . . . just because some people abuse them, they should not be regulated. I believe in the market. There is enough competition. The risky credit card person has to pay more interest. That's also a discipline, like getting insurance.

She has firm feelings about those who get into trouble, although she doesn't know anyone personally:

Do you know anyone who pays interest? I don't know anyone, or at least they don't talk about it. Our friends are all so careful. There are lots of reasons to be overextended: investing, gambling, getting sick. Some people in this generation abuse it, and eventually they have to pay the piper . . . they lose their credit rating or go bankrupt. They don't really know, but eventually people will realize that there are consequences. Some people can't do anything, like compulsive shoppers; they lose their credit card or find someone to subsidize them, like a husband or something.

Finally, Smith has a possibly contradictory, but sturdy sense of why other people charge: "You can use credit and keep your money in the bank. Why should I subsidize all the credit card users by paying cash? They're getting the use of that money (by charging) and you're not."

Madeline Smith articulates the feelings of many Americans, which has come to constitute a kind of moral divide between people who pay interest and people who do not. She believes that people must take personal responsibility for credit and debt. Those who abuse debt suffer from some ailment such as drug addiction or a flawed character. Parents must teach children to use debt wisely. An unregulated market can take care of the problem if they do not, with the rightful consequence that they will be asked to "pay the piper." She articulates these views from the social position of someone who uses credit cards carefully, who can still afford a frugal, but gourmet life that takes nice things for granted, and who believes that she doesn't know any people who show signs of irresponsible use. She feels that those who carry an interest-bearing balance are in personal trouble. She believes that charging but paying off the balance before interest accrues keeps her in step with those others who do the same thing.

She represents a generation that endured the Depression and World War II, but enjoyed a healthy postwar economy, the benefits of the GI Bill that privileged mostly white men, and healthy mortgage assistance programs provided by the Veterans Administration and the Federal Housing Administration. She expressed mild annoyance at being part of the pioneer generation of white middle-class women who had to go to work outside the home. With the stretch her income provided, her family enjoyed a comfortable standard of living and freedom from debt. Her grown children have had access to the least expensive credit around.[37]

Smith enjoys the board game "Monopoly." Anthropologist Penelope Mitchell argues that the game, created during the Depression era, "offered players an opportunity to be a part of the future by investing their money in solid, income-generating real estate." In contrast, Mitchell writes, the 1990s game "Mall Madness" offers "an opportunity to shop to our heart's content without ever feeling the pangs of debt." Whereas in Monopoly "players get money from investments, luck, and work . . . in Mall Madness money is received simply by going to the bank. You receive money through inserting a credit card into a machine that decides whimsically whether or not to give it to you. You win by being the first player to purchase six different items and then return to the parking lot." Madeline Smith never bought this game. All her life she has used credit responsibly, following the rules established by her generation that continue to make sense to her. She feels rightly proud of her sensible use of credit, for she has not done anything wrong. But she may slight or not really understand the more difficult experiences of those who followed her past "Go" in less auspicious times.[38]

Smith exemplifies the first group of customers sought by retail banks in the late 1970s. The Equal Credit Opportunity Act guaranteed her the right to her own credit, even though she was married and a mother. Emboldened by the Marquette decision, by their own new screening and authorization technology, and reeling from losses on Third World loans and overbuilt suburban real estate, the financial services industry labored hard to identify and sign on creditworthy customers. Ironically, a time of deep recession and distress became a frenzied period of experimentation, competition, and growth for the retail banking industry, and especially for its credit card divisions. But those who had been good savings customers were simply not good credit card customers, and this took bankers by surprise. Like Madeline Smith, most bank cardholders' initial forays into the credit card economy were for convenience, and most paid off their monthly purchases or maintained only a modest balance.

Consider banks' sources of credit card revenue. To reap profit from their loans, they relied on annual "membership" fees, the interest fees they charged on rolled-over balances to customers who did not pay the whole bill each month, and the penalties they charged customers who exceeded their credit limit or made late payments. They "bundled" their cards (so they could not be seen?) with checking accounts and overdraft protection in varied idioms of "relationship banking." They sold their lists of customers to other businesses, and they hawked the backs of their billing and return envelopes to advertisers. Bankers also charged merchants "discount" fees of 3–4 percent for the goods and services they sold to credit card customers. As inflation climbed, they increased the fees that merchants had to pay. Banks also experimented with more thorough and deceptive ways of calculating interest, moving from the adjusted balance method (which calculates interest at the time payment is due) to the average daily balance system (which figures interest from the time the purchase is made). But ultimately they had to confront the problem of conservative, comfortable customers like Smith. These carefully screened, creditworthy customers whom banks had worked so hard to attract were problematic: they paid on time and thus rode free, paying no interest at all. The cost of soliciting hesitant, suspicious customers, keeping records, and corresponding with merchants seemed too heavy a burden to carry; credit cards were more trouble than they were worth.

Customers like Madeline Smith deprived banks of interest income, late payment charges, and over-the-limit fees. Banks soon turned against these careful users, labeling them "convenience users" and claiming to suffer at the hands of those who had, in fact, "used credit cards the way they were originally intended." A sound credit card portfolio, one banker argued, should include no more than 25–30 percent "deadbeats" like Smith.[39] Their options seemed clear: increase the number of interest-paying debtors, dump the deadbeats. In hindsight, one wonders why bankers could not have simply told convenience users, "This is free credit, and it costs money." Instead the ideology of free credit for some, high interest for others, began to take root. In the next chapter, I will turn to the experiences and perspectives of those who pay interest. But in concluding this chapter, I will bring the story of convenience users up to date by focusing on how they continue to thwart banks.

The Plague of the Deadbeats

One strategy for dealing with convenience users has been to try to persuade them to charge more. Surely, eventually, they would be forced to pay interest. Visa and MasterCard packaged collaborations with affinity groups like university alumni, clubs, churches, political parties, the socially conscious, athletes, wilderness enthusiasts, Elvis fans, and even people with the same astrological sign or surname. "For Every Williams . . . A Card of Distinction. Your FamilyCard brings the pride of your historic lineage into your daily life."[40]

In 1987 credit card issuers began to emphasize such tie-ins to encourage convenience users to use their cards more often: "More money for the way you really live." Visa teamed up with the Hilton Hotel Chain and the American Automobile Association, and everybody found a frequent flier friend who would offer airline miles in exchange for dollars spent. By 1993, passengers had racked up 1.8 trillion frequent flier miles. Citibank rewarded heavy users with bonus "dollars" toward selected brand-name merchandise; Bank of America offered a prepaid legal service. These tie-in, rebate, affinity, and co-branding strategies continued to rage in the 1990s, as MasterCard partnered with General Motors, AT&T with General Electric, NationsBank with Blockbuster Video, First USA with Hertz, and Chemical Bank with Shell Oil to offer rebates on gasoline and vacation packages. MasterCard advertising director Jim Desrosier mused in Adweek that "consumers have a warmer feeling for pizza than for banks. If a pizza theme attached to a card gets them to use it more, then it is a good idea."[41] MBNA offered free hotel nights and emergency roadside service. Chevy Chase Bank offered a free camera to customers who would try out their home improvement services. Visa offered customers the chance to win a trip to the Olympic Summer Games in return for their willingness to charge from such merchants as KAY-BEE, Chili's, and Circuit City. In 1996 the "Dining a la Card" program allowed diners to eat at their favorite restaurants and receive 20 percent cash back automatically simply for charging.

For convenience users the annual fee and annual percentage rate seemed increasingly irrelevant, because they paid no interest but gained many perks and even made money on their cards. Buying thousands of free airline miles for a $50.00 annual fee seemed cheap. A New York Times advertisement for Visa featured a beautiful bouquet of long-stemmed roses and asked the question: "Was he sorry? Or was it the miles?" One hearty convenience user showed me a summer contest she was entering, for which she wrote fifty words describing the miles she had charged: the most romantic, the most ordinary, and the most humanitarian. If she won the contest, she would win more and more miles, helping to fill the skies with convenience users. My brother described to me traveling around the world on free credit when, as he put it, "My credit card was home." In 1997 the American Airlines Advantage Program offered customers the chance to donate $50 to the National Park Foundation's "Miles for Trails" program in exchange for 500 free airline miles.

Affinity strategies worked well. The rewards induced cardholders to charge nearly twice as much and twice as often as people who were not eligible for them. Convenience users began to earn hundreds of dollars every year in perks, way more than the credit card companies had expected. "They track their reward points like a stock portfolio, search for program loopholes to maximize their profits and turbocharge their monthly statements with imaginative new uses, from college tuition to the monthly mortgage . . . beating credit-card companies at their own game . . . If you can't charge it, don't buy it."[42] People bounded from card to card, earning rewards with each hop, letting friends use their cards to pile up airline tickets and telephone credits.

By 2000 Web pages shared tips about reward programs. If the company required you to carry a balance to receive a rebate, people tried revolving $1.00. If they hit their maximum, they shifted to other cards to rack up prizes. One man rented five cars in one day to get a quick free airline ticket. Then to earn double bonus miles he charged $10,000 worth of computer equipment for friends who paid him back in cash. Credit card companies did not make money on such people.

Today some convenience users have transformed themselves into "megachargers" who profit from co-branding and rebate strategies by charging *everything*. Quintessential megacharger Howard Means describes this strategy vividly:

It looks like an indictment—15 single-spaced pages from Citibank, documenting every expenditure my wife and I made last year on our Advantage credit card. The $43.50 I spent to play nine holes of bad golf on a rain-drenched course in Pennsylvania, for example. Line after line of double-digit and triple-digit tabs from Giant Food, Fresh Fields, Nordstrom, the Hecht Company, Hechinger, CHS, Exxon, Texaco. Payments to physicians, dentists, hairdressers. Grand excesses flash before my eyes: $249.20 for a wonderful meal with old friends on Manhattan's East Side, two tickets to a Kennedy Center opera. So do the small gestures that leaven this compulsive consumption, like the $35 contribution to WAMU-FM.

Then there are the four really big charges: Two payments to the cashier of my son's university, the other two to the finance office at my daughter's college. When push came to shove in the great college tuition battle, my wife and I did the American thing: We said, "Charge it!"

Thus co-branding and rebate strategies were remarkably successful in wooing those suspicious of credit at all as well as those who might otherwise have charged less frequently. But they had two dire consequences, one for many citizens and the other for banks. They fueled the credit inequality that is the hallmark of the consumer credit card system by allowing some to profit, while others paid interest and lost money on credit cards. By 1997 bankers appeared thoroughly tired of the convenience user/megachargers who were costing them more money than they had anticipated.[43]

Analysts in the $400 billion industry worried about what to do. Their frequent flier miles and automobile programs were effective but stale and cluttered. Other companies easily copied cash rebates. But the truly harsh downside of these enhancements was that convenience users used them "so the yield from them can suffer." Thus, the banks capped benefits, closed loopholes, slapped on maintenance fees, and tried to weed out card sharks. But even the "mature market" of interest-paying debtors was saturated, even declining by the early 1990s. Desperate for new marketing strategies, the industry pondered what to do. In Chapter 4 we will see what they did.[44]

But in 1999 financial institutions were *still* taking a bath on rebates, and convenience use was getting worse, rising from 29 percent in 1990 to 42 percent in 1999, partly because some people were able to pay off their credit card loans by changing to a company with lower interest. They had been hoist by their own petards.[45] "Co-Branded" cards seemed to languish until the end of 2003. By this time the market was clotted with more than 620 million cards in use, double the number in 1992. Searching for a distinctive card, Starbucks, Bank One Corp., and Visa USA launched the Duetto card, and a credit card researcher Robert McKinley quipped, "I'm sure there will be a Krispy Kreme Visa at some point, too."[46]

In this climate, Madeline Smith, the original and careful cardholder, seems outdated and undone, her symbolic descendants split into those card sharks who profited from airline and auto miles and those who paid interest, lots of it. In the next chapter, I explore bankers' turn to those customers who would pay interest and to the experiences and perceptions of the people termed "revolvers."

Chapter 3

Rustling Up Revolvers

The world faced another oil crisis in 1979. The oil-producing nations with-held oil again, prices leapt, and inflation spread around the world. High prices in turn slowed sales of the world's products and brought unemploy-ment and recession. Some of the developing nations could no longer pay interest on the loans they owed to American banks. Banks were in trouble, and they pressed the government for help. Because inflation was boosting prices, credit was no longer profitable. The government provided relief: under President Reagan, the interest rates that bankers had to pay for money they borrowed from the central bank dropped from 16 percent to 7 percent in just a few years. By 1992 it was only 3 percent. These drops in the discount rate made the spread between federal reserve borrowing and credit card lending much more profitable.

Banks rallied with energetic marketing efforts aimed at increasing credit card loans, searching for revolvers (those borrowers who maintained a bal-ance), and imposing a creative plague of penalty fees for every little malfea-sance imaginable. With some nations' loans in default, and monstrous developments sitting like beached whales in the suburbs, credit cards be-came banks' chief source of profit.[1]

Bankers settled into a long-term, mostly unsuccessful struggle to mine profits from convenience users (those who paid off their balances each month). But the industry had to revise its standards of creditworthiness to build portfolios of heavily burdened people, who, though bowed with debt, faithfully paid interest each month. This search for potential debtors was executed by the retail banking industry and economists from the Federal Reserve Board. They asked: Who uses credit cards? What do they do with them? How do they feel about them? Do they pay in full? If not, do they pay interest faithfully? What distinguishes a convenience user from an in-stallment user, a nonrevolver from a revolver? How can we profit from both? Or, just in case, how can we turn the one into the other?

At first, bankers fretted about how they could minimize the risks that revolvers would pose. Who was most likely to default? Was occupation a powerful predictor? One early conclusion was, "yes": beware of drivers, laborers, and those employed in manufacturing, construction, retail, and wholesale trade. Your better customers include people in banking, finance, and real estate. These discoveries seemed to echo the shift in the American economy from manufacturing to services, especially financial services.[2]

In 1983 the Federal Reserve Board (FRB), on behalf of seven federal agencies, began to publish the findings of a long-term study commissioned at the University of Michigan, which would shape credit card outreach for the next ten years. These articles sought to help retail bankers snare debtors and were published frequently in the *Journal of Retail Banking*. For example, in 1985, FRB staff economists Canner and Cyrnak wrote:

> Comparison of credit card holding and use patterns among families over time provides an opportunity to evaluate both the level of and changes in credit card *penetration* rates among families grouped by similar demographic and financial characteristics. Card issuers, such as banks and retailers, will find this type of data useful for comparison with their own credit card operations. *In particular, they may use it in identifying market segments to target for solicitation.* (emphasis added)[3]

What distinguished convenience users, still 50 percent of the credit card holding population in 1983, from installment users? Canner and Cyrnak informed their readers that convenience users held more ready money and managed more diverse finances. They were better educated, disliked carrying cash, valued clear records, and occasionally needed a short-term bridge between purchase and paycheck. Sometimes the two could cross over: convenience users might charge an especially expensive item, and pay it off in installments, and revolvers might pay off a balance with, say, a large tax refund. But most customers were "essentially one or the other."[4]

In 1986, Canner and Cyrnak continued their work for the Association of Retail Banking, alarmed by the national debate on usury (placing a cap on the interest rates banks could charge). Canner and Cyrnak wrote that their research "will help issuers increase interest income and contribute to the debate on a national ceiling." They explained that convenience users used bankcards to free up cash in the bank, as Madeline Smith suggests, because of the grace period between purchase and payment. Some convenience users found checks *in*convenient or unacceptable. Many liked to collect a receipt for proof of purchase, because they expected to be reimbursed or because they liked leverage in returning merchandise or resolving a dispute. To convenience users, credit meant power.

Therefore, Canner and Cyrnak argued, issuers needed to make changes to increase their credit-related revenue. They needed to expand credit limits to tempt customers to buy items so expensive they would *have* to revolve the balance. They should target the highest-income families with premium cards and, conversely, expand their reach to more essential products and services such as utility bills and insurance premiums to trap those who still felt ambivalent about charging. Most importantly, issuers needed to create a tiered system offering different terms for customers who bundled services such as a credit card and a checking account as opposed to those who did not, or for those who carried little or no balance against those who did.[5]

The industry's *Journal of Retail Banking* unabashedly advised its readers in the winter of 1987–88: "Fortunately for retail banks, there is *still* significant debt capacity in the consumer market, even though some segments of it are already overstretched. Indeed, the level of consumer indebtedness appears to be alarmingly high in relation to household income."[6] Concerned about write-offs and out-of-date and overburdened credit scoring procedures, the journal lamented banks' tendency

to solicit new accounts from ever-lower socioeconomic segments of the market instead of further penetrating the increased debt capacities of more attractive customers. Banks have to find new and creative ways to stimulate demand from the "right," underleveraged consumers, those who can afford to maintain or expand indebtedness, possibly by stimulating impulse driven access at the point of purchase.[7]

Pursuing these ignoble goals to drag into debt those who could bear up under a little more, banks were mightily aggressive: Theresa Sullivan, Elizabeth Warren, and Jay Westbrook write of banks' campaigns: "The stories of excessive credit extension abound, including the pussy cat in Ohio who got a credit card in the mail, the inmates at a state prison who all got credit cards because they had stable addresses, and the fellow in Dallas who went home from the foreclosure sale on his house to find waiting for him a new $5,000 Gold MasterCard."[8]

Throughout the decade, bankers reminded each other of the lessons they learned in the watershed period of the early 1980s: the best customers are not those who are the best credit risks. They divided credit card users into three types: people who pay their bills each month and are never charged interest, people who intend to pay their bills but at the end of the month cannot quite manage, and people who run up bills knowing full well they cannot afford them. "The middle group is where the profit is for the banks."[9]

Bankers also pursued a specialized marketing niche: the "aging baby boomer." Aging baby boomers "buy more and save less than any other generation; they spend on products other generations would have considered luxuries, like electronics, second cars, and household services. . . . The heart of growth and profitability in bankcards—because of high usage and extended time of repayment—is the quality products that are aesthetically pleasing, personally satisfying, natural, and non-caloric."[10]

Banks must appeal "to the sybaritic lifestyle—being good to myself—the new narcissism." Another feature of the baby boomers' lifestyle is "time poverty," which could be exploited through "time-using products and services, like tennis equipment, RV's, boats, recreational condos, and vacations." This may seem contradictory, but the journal rationalized that boomers perceived themselves as having little time. They were therefore willing to pay for better quality goods and services to make the most of that little time. A second strategy was to provide "time-saving goods and services," through ATMs, convenience stores, catalogues, or even eliminating banks through home-computer banking. Fortunately "baby boomers do not pay their bills on time because they do not have the time."

"Baby boomers delayed getting married and having children, but they did not reject the institution of marriage or the instrument that facilitates marriage: the credit card." Profitability for banks increased with the couples' procreation. "The production of children produces an increased need for plastic transactions. Among other things, children need clothes, shoes, school supplies, and food. Their parents need credit." Also, there were more "first-order babies" around, and "first-order babies generate twice as many sales as second and subsequent babies." Finally, the boomers' tendency to have fewer babies later in life meant that they bought higher quality products. They valued style and attractiveness more than durability because there were fewer hand-me-downs involved.[11]

Despite their foolish stereotypes, bankers have been enormously successful at signing up this generation, who faced a polarized economy, downward mobility, and hard choices. "We had to choose between kids, houses, and time," writes Katy Butler, conceding the role of the credit card in "the disguised slide down." So often accused of being unable to defer gratification, many have deferred what their parents considered basic. "As people dispossessed from housing and family life have done before, they wore their fortunes on their backs or sunk them into their cars. . . . The $200 that paid our parents' mortgages would only cover our car payments; but we bought Land's End instead of Sears, and learned to call noodles and coffee 'fettuccine' and 'cappuccino,' coping by running up credit card debt to keep up appearances.[12]

By 1984 banks had soared out of their 1980 malaise. Unpaid credit loans grew from $300 billion in 1980 to $795 billion in 1990, and for the lenders this was good news. Michael Perry was trapped. He succumbed to personal debt, in part because he is a baby boomer. He suffered from the occupational changes that displaced and devalued many workers, and he was part of a labor market glutted with workers whose resources had shrunk. His problems were exacerbated by various life cycle squeezes: setting up a household that demanded major purchases, growing poorer after a divorce. His story reveals remorse about his mistakes, a dogged effort to maintain a middle-class standard of living, and the horrible anxiety of living with debt.

I asked Michael to write his own story for this chapter. He is thoughtful and articulate, with strong feelings about credit cards. Although Michael has strong feelings, his experiences are similar to those of many other people who were lured into debt during the 1980s. His credit card debt may reflect some bad choices, but it also reflects a changing economy and his bouts with unemployment. He wrote the first part of his story while looking for work, when he felt terribly harried by creditors.

MICHAEL'S STORY

I got my first credit card in 1980. My parents had added me as a co-debtor to their cards. When they died, the credit simply transferred over to me. It seemed like a great opportunity to buy things without a thought to the consequences of debt. I'd had no briefing or instruction on their use by Mom and Dad, and I used it freely.

They [the credit card companies] play upon people's wishes to become somehow better than they are led to believe by the advertising media conglomerate. Playing to people's baser instincts to become happy, somehow, through the accumulation of things . . . to provide temporary relief from the stresses and strains of living in a society that is so totally out of whack with personal values and personal development. There was never a real "need" to use a card. Only the temptation to buy things I thought would somehow augment my status in the eyes of others. I fell, hook, line, and sinker, into the deal and bet my future against present wants. I am sorry that I have fallen prey to my own desire to become like the others. However, I pay and pay and pay.

My first real *need* to use a credit card was when I lost my job in the recession of 1990. I had just bought my first house—a condo, actually—and two or three months later, the company I was working for went out of business. I used [the credit card] for cash advances to pay my newly acquired mortgage and utility bills, when in June, our paychecks started bouncing. Notices from the health-care plan came, informing us [my girlfriend and me] that we no longer had benefits. My girlfriend and I suddenly found ourselves strapped. I'd just bought a new truck and co-signed a car loan for her. It was awful.

I started selling off the things I'd purchased . . . things I thought would make our house comfortable for us. She sold her diamond ring from a previous marriage, to pay a month's mortgage. None of the things I purchased have outlasted the debt. Instead, I found myself paying for a color TV that I sold at a yard sale when I lost my job, in order to pay my mortgage. I think the guy who came to look at it offered me fifty bucks, and I took it. I was so desperate. I even helped him carry it down the stairs to his car.

I'd been left with maybe 8 or 10 thousand dollars of debt. Mostly cash advances to pay the mortgage. Which ultimately did not work, because the bank foreclosed and I lost the house. I used the credit cards to buy groceries, hoping, in my soul, that I would be able to recoup the debt. I worked as an independent computer analyst, knocking on doors, soliciting whatever work I could find. Barely enough to pay the bills. I used the credit cards to pay for the truck and her car, hoping that, somehow, things would turn around. But they didn't, and I found myself unable to support the burden of debt, and, on more than one occasion, considered blowing my head off with the Taurus revolver I'd bought, on credit, for personal protection.

I managed eventually to find somewhat more stable employment as a subcontractor working in, of all places, a bank. How the bankruptcy I had on my credit record slid by when they did the credit check is beyond me. Apparently bankruptcy is now acceptable, because after a year or so of steady employment I was offered credit cards with beginner's limits. Providian was the first to offer, and now feeling fiscally competent and responsible, I decided to take them up on it. The rate was horrible. Twenty-two percent interest. But I vowed to use the card only for emergencies thinking that by having a card I would be able to reestablish my credit.

Once I burst the bubble, I allowed myself to buy, of all things, a color TV (oh God, not again!) and a stereo system because I no longer felt it was economically feasible to rent from Rent-A-Center at their exorbitant weekly rates. I bought those items because I was attempting to display my "affluence" to whomever would stop by my little rented house. That they would see that I was part of the American culture.

Today I have five cards. Two with Capital One, two with Providian, one of which was transferred to a company called eMerge, which is basically a collection agency that Providian reluctantly admits is part of its own organization. I'd been paying my bills on time, and have no idea why they "sold" my credit line to eMerge. Nevertheless they sold it and I am now being billed at a fantastic 29 percent rate.

I was unaware of this transaction because unfamiliar envelopes began appearing in the mail from a company I'd never heard of—eMerge! On the surface they appeared to be just another solicitation for yet another credit card. Those envelopes got tossed, unopened, into the trash along with the jam of junk mail that appears in my box unsolicited.

That, in itself, is a complete story, involving late fees, overlimit fees and the whole gamut of dunning. I have a fifth card with Axys Bank, which is a card provided by Fingerhut. It is, nevertheless, a credit card, and I am sorry for having used it to buy furniture (I was using the box from the color TV for a coffee table) to complete the middle-class concept of accessorizing my new digs.

I have resisted the temptation to acquire other cards, even though now I still get offers in the mail at least twice a month. I stopped using all the cards last October

[2002], if not before, when I realized things were getting out of control. Now I only make payments.

When I first had credit, I would pay off the full amount. As things got worse, due to unemployment, I'd pay the minimum. I'd always try and be on time, but as the 1990s came to an end and I struggled to keep up with truly important expenses (rent, electricity), late fees and overlimit fees kept pushing the balance way beyond the max.

I've missed payments because I've had to pay the rent. I've missed payments because I've had major car repairs. I've missed payments because the heating bill in the winter was almost beyond my means. I've missed payments because I've been deluged by mail from creditors and, unable to cope with the amounts due, tried to set priority to payments.

I spend a good portion of my day worrying about paying my bills and constantly checking my bank account balance . . . creating spreadsheets to project my payments. . . . Frankly, I spend an inordinate amount of time obsessing about how I can dig myself out of this hole.

I attempt to spend my money carefully and essentially, base my daily needs against the money I'll need to pay to keep myself out of paying late fees and overlimit fees.

I have to balance my budget almost to the day, sometimes beyond, to keep from having my phone cut off. To keep my car from being repossessed. To keep from being ejected from my home because I'm short on rent money. To pay the electric bill. I keep a close watch on when my direct deposit will be made, so I can "float" a payment in time for the deposit to cover a deadline payment to someone. It's like I spend half of my waking life, if not more, paying and paying and paying.

I know I have made some bad decisions in my life. And now I pay. But the creditors are relentless—

From my point of view, they dig and dig and dig. A knife dug into my gut until I cry, "Yes, yes, yes, I'll pay!" What burns me is the fees. The overlimit fees that push me even further down into a crevasse from which I see little hope of returning. Unless I get some kind of miraculous job that will pay me what I'm worth.

I am so tired of being hit on by these people. It exhausts me. My mind is totally frazzled by their continued browbeating to extract from me something that they make me feel like is my own fault. In a legal sense, it is my own doing. But Jesus God, will they ever let up? I did not intend to get into debt like this. I am so angry, because I want to do the right thing. But they just seem to keep coming on in waves of force sucking the life-blood out of my soul so that I can't concentrate on anything else. Every day is an awakening to my debt.

They want only one thing, and that is their money. Period. I used to get called all the time because, being unemployed, I could not make my payments. I'd try and work out payments, but my income at the time was only $328 a week, and the rent, utilities, and car payments took priority. I was stretched to the max. But, bit by bit, I've managed to get back on track with at least keeping up with the minimums.

Some of them stop at nothing and use some very heavy-handed strong-arm tactics to extract the money. They threaten, and I've been called at work when I was employed. I've had to sneak into unoccupied offices at work to return calls and make arrangements because the cube I worked in was not private enough. Everyone around would have been able to hear my plight and begging. They usually use a tactic wherein they threaten legal action and demand payment immediately. It takes many calls and stretching of the budget to resolve the issues. I have documentation in my many files to prove this.

But they are the ones in power, not me.

In sublime irony, during the summer of 2003, Michael got temporary work at a credit card company. This is the essay he wrote about it:

I entered Riker's Island at 6 P.M. The room was furnished with a large mahogany conference table, BetaPhone centered on its highly polished surface. Charcoal grey broadcloth computer chairs surrounded it, emblazoned with graphic designs of handcuffs, jail cell bars, and padlocks.

Not an altogether uncomfortable environment, excluding, of course, the video surveillance cameras and audio pickups mounted in the corners. My discomfort was not particularly dispelled considering the names of the fifteen or so other conference and "huddle rooms . . . Alcatraz, Leavenworth, Belle Isle. I considered the last for a moment thinking of the bright and up-and-coming designer who came up with that one.

"Had to be a Richmonder," I thought. Who else would know about the Civil War island on the James River where so many Union prisoners had seen their last days exposed in an outdoor prison camp sharing cholera and dysentery with their fellow inmates?

My reverie burst, I came back to reality, and I settled in for another long night of hardware hookups and software configurations.

"OK guys, the hardware's not here yet, but we can go ahead and get started on the Plan As." The general announcement commenced our activities for the evening.

Cut sheets were grouped according to cube locations and assigned to each of the five of us. Technicians, all but one, with years of experience, having come from well-paying jobs that had somehow dissolved into the abyss of creeping economic downturn. We were in the bowels of the very system that had caused our plight. Earning half, if not less, than we had in our previous positions. But at least we were off unemployment for a while . . . who knew exactly how long the contract would last? Supposedly through the entire summer. Maybe on into the fall. A golden opportunity to work at a discount and earn enough money to keep up with the minimum balances on our credit cards.

It was an employer's market now, and the glory of being a computer analyst had faded. The market was glutted with millions of out-of-work techs, some unemployed for a year or longer. We were at least lucky enough to have been hired for this particular contract. Something to work with when fending off those persistent calls from creditors, but just barely. I could not help but feel I was treading water . . . drowning in the undertow of debt.

It's not like I'd been extravagant. Just the basics of the American way of life. A small (very small) house that I rent, a seven-year-old car, and the various insurance policies required (by law!) to maintain them. No porterhouse steaks or Armani suits. Hell, even bread was nearly $3 a loaf for anything with nutritional value. That was the one thing I tried to keep up with. Nutrition. Without health insurance any longer, it was even important to maintain good health. And the stress of the job (the hours were a God-awful third shift) ensured that every calorie would be used to the fullest.

The work was not physically grueling. Just lifting a few monitors and moving some CPUs around. I hadn't been prepared for the toll that stress would take because of the 180-degree turn in the workday. It was more than just a lifestyle disruption, coming in at 6 P.M. and leaving anywhere between 2 A.M. and 5 A.M. My whole body clock completely rejected the flip, making it impossible to get any real sleep. Even with the blinds closed and curtains drawn, even after the most exhausting nights, I could only sleep in snippets of two or three hours.

The funny thing is, we were thankful to be employed and earning enough to keep our heads above water. Once into the actual work all other thoughts become muted. Working under the 5 A.M. deadline (with success quotas) there was little time to focus on anything other than technical details. And there were plenty of those.

A certain camaraderie developed. At least among the six members of our team. The various users would not have appreciated some of our comments as we joked about which ones spent time shopping on the Internet during business hours. One could not ignore the lists of Web site cookies that would display during file transfers. Not to mention the volume of MP3, video files, chain letters, and jokes. What exactly did some of these people do all day?

This was of little concern to us, other than the fact that the incredible volume of useless information bogged down the transfer system. It only made our nights longer. Sometimes hours waiting for files to copy up to the server and back down again.

Fortunately there were perks to keep us going. Chocolate and other candies presented appreciatively in bowls at various cubes. Coupled with the free coffee in the galley our heads were buzzingly anxious to get these machines upgraded and working! On a good night, we could come across a spread of food left over from a meeting. Cakes, cold cuts, crackers, donuts, bread and rolls. . . .

Unfortunately, the only light at the end of the tunnel is a lack of long-term job security. This project will come to an end along with all its perks, lousy hours, slacker users, and miscommunications. It could come at any time. Someone could fuck up royally, and Capital One could decide to terminate the contract. Or it could just come to term, and the top-rated employer in Virginia will be fully migrated from old technology to new.

In either case, I have found that, relying on the old idea that working hard and maintaining loyalty has no effect on those at the top of the food chain. After all, people like me are a dime a dozen, and there's always someone else knocking at the door for the opportunity to work, pay bills, and have a little left over for a movie or time with one's family.

I think the repulsiveness of this job is taking a toll on me. It goes so totally against my ethic. I think, for the moment, I am too close to the forest to really see how best to determine my position. On one hand I'm very angry with myself for prostituting myself for the very same type of organization that has enticed me into debt. These people, whoever they are, are evil and stop at nothing to extract money from anyone they can possibly touch. They will stop at nothing to suck out the life of people who, for the most part, I think, are just trying to get by. They have no morals and I honestly think they are leeches . . . but, unlike a leech, they cannot be simply plucked off and tossed back into the swamp in which they breed. For example: the other night I overheard one "customer service rep" talking to a client. His purpose was to reconcile the victim's account and, if at all possible within "legal" means, extract from them whatever payment possible. He was smooth and chatty. He led his victim into a conversation that, seemingly, was one of concern for their financial plight. He asked questions about her current job, location, and bank account information. He provided what appeared on the surface to be sympathy for her condition, but the underlying structure was to glean as much information as possible to screw that person out of whatever funds she had in her bank account. He was talking with the victim about how her job was going, how she was getting along with her husband, and if she liked the house she was living in. The kicker is, he was sitting back in his chair, headset in place, keying in every bit of information about her into his computer. Trust me, there was no compassion on his part. Once he had made payment arrangements with her, he clicked on an icon on his computer screen and called yet another person to lead down the garden path.

There is also a list . . called POISN . . . reserved for people who cannot pay. . . . These are the people who are dunned to death. The bottom line of the list has a section called "hardball" and referred to procedures leading to prosecution of these people. The whole place is nothing more than a factory for extorting money from people.

The contract is coming to a close on the 20th, so they are pushing to get as much stuff done as possible. And in their rush, they are screwing up bigtime. The work orders, known to us as "cut-sheets," are all messed up and we, on the front lines of computer reintegration, have to make up for their lack of attention to detail.

Needless to say, this makes for frustrating and mentally, as well as physically (involving moving computer equipment from floor to floor), exhausting conditions. I have been doing this kind of work for over eighteen years, and, to see the lack of organization these people put into their efforts makes me . . . sick.

Michael's deep frustration as he seeks work in the expanding financial services sector while negotiating with creditors from that same sector will resonate with many people in debt. His experience as a redundant computer analyst echoes that of many people who have coped with unemployment.

Experiencing Debt

Why have so many American households fallen into serious credit card debt? In what is still one of the best reports on credit and debt, Robert Pollin demonstrates convincingly what he calls the "necessitous demand" that led households to borrow so much in the 1980s. Wages fell by 12.4 percent between 1972 and 1988, and incomes fell even more. American society was growing more unequal, as service jobs replaced manufacturing jobs that went overseas. Although surveys consistently showed that consumers thought installment buying was bad, they still borrowed. Different households borrowed for different reasons: wealthier people borrowed to speculate, while poorer people borrowed to make ends meet, not because they were sanguine about going into debt. Lower income people spent a higher percentage of their income on housing. Pollin shows that although housing prices rose, people were not buying new or more expensive homes. By 1988 only 15.8 percent of homes sold were new. Housing costs varied in different parts of the country. They were highest in those places still offering decent job opportunities, and many people had to relocate to those places. As people relocated to work, they had to buy those more expensive homes. Housing is the least flexible item in the family budget, so with more resources directed to financing housing, families had less available for other expenses. People made many adjustments to their loss of income. In addition to accepting smaller homes, they reduced savings, postponed marriages and children, borrowed more from their relatives, and, yes, leaned more on credit card debt.[13]

Personal debt reflects the ravages and inequalities of the 1980s and people's desperate, sometimes misguided, often inescapable efforts to maintain the illusion of a middle-class standard of living that was in fact plummeting. They borrow to make ends meet. Women have been especially vulnerable, because of relatively low salaries and gendered mobility ladders, the high costs of child care and health insurance, and their lowered incomes after widowhood or divorce. Some people in their middle years have been able to call on older relatives who did well during the postwar boom, but for others credit cards have increasingly served as welfare, domestic partners, and the community chest.

Often credit card debt is linked to the pressures of the life cycle. Young people launching households may earn very little yet expect to fill their homes with some of the material objects that to them symbolize the transition to an adult life.[14] Since the mid-1980s, credit card issuers have eagerly sought such new householders as customers. One young couple whom I interviewed had accumulated $19,000 in debt before either had turned nineteen in 1990. They no longer charge, but believe that their service sector jobs may never allow them to pay their way out of a situation that is ruefully reminiscent of debt peonage. The same thing happened to a young man who moved to Atlanta in 1985 to work in the corrections system there. By 1987 he had accumulated more than $20,000 of credit card debt, which he had used to set up an apartment and buy clothes. By the time he realized how overextended he had become, his creditors were harassing him at work and scaring him badly. Reporter Tobias told of how Anita Behrens, with three children and a $5.00 an hour job, enrolled in junior college so that she could eventually make more money. She borrowed from credit cards to pay tuition, buy diapers and a used car, to treat her children. Eventually she was using most of her payments from AFDC (Aid to Families with Dependent Children) to pay credit card interest. She finally declared bankruptcy owing $64,000 in debt.[15]

For those able to buy a house, the mortgage can become an albatross. As one woman put it, her family fought to "keep up appearances while we were unable to eat nutritiously . . . making those (mortgage) payments and charging everything else."

These problems are exacerbated for households with children. One man talked of his "credit card baby," because he had no health insurance. New babies are expensive, as are teenagers, who may reach adolescence just as their relatives' earnings are flattening out. Many people have taken on debt to fight for upward mobility or middle-class advantages for their children.

Middle-class comfort and ease can be financed by many only on the installment plan. Former middle-class entitlements have become prohibitively expensive. Families are increasingly unable to save to pay for a house, a car, or a college education and must therefore borrow to do so. Many people have used credit cards to ensure their families some of the perks of a middle-class lifestyle: braces, designer glasses, piano lessons, holidays, birthday presents, summer enrichment, new clothes for school. One woman sent all three of her children through college on cash advances, and many universities today allow students to charge their tuition. Thus, rather than symbolizing an inability to defer gratification, credit card debt is made to seem more like an investment in the future. And when the future doesn't work out as planned, American households more and more frequently house friends and relatives who cannot afford to live on their own, along with boomerang kids who move back in with them after being unable to find good jobs. As households wax, wane, and dissolve, as members face disruptions such as death, separation, divorce, the arrival or departure of friends and kin, the birth of children, disease, or disability, credit cards help them stretch and pool.

In addition, Americans found by the mid-1980s that they had smaller cushions with which to manage expected and unexpected large bills: car insurance or car repairs, a stove or washing machine to replace one that gave out, a leaking roof. They have used credit cards to weather all sorts of emergencies. As cards' possible uses increased, people paid doctors', dentists', and veterinarians' bills and bought medicines and groceries, all with credit cards. One therapist I interviewed, who specializes in helping people with debt addictions, confessed to accepting credit cards! In the public sector you can now charge postage stamps, pay property and income taxes, parking and speeding tickets, motor vehicle fees, and even civil penalties. Credit cards are especially important in times of income interruption, for not everyone is eligible for unemployment compensation, and even if you are, it is woefully inadequate. Also, many people who have lost their jobs find new ones that pay much less. One man, the father of two small children, lost a restaurant job at a seafood house where he had worked for ten years. Manager and main chef, he worked ten hours a day, six days a week, paid partly over and partly under the table. He made about $500 a week. When the owner sold the restaurant, this experienced man was forced into the more anonymous service sector, and even then he ended up at a restaurant that after three years asked him and the entire staff to take a pay cut. He left to accept minimum wage working at a shelter for ill, homeless men. He never approached his former salary and was forced to use credit cards to pay for food and clothing for his family.

Contrary to stereotypes about selfish, greedy consumers, many people fell into debt helping others. One young woman, supporting herself on a teacher's salary, moved in with a domestic worker and her three sons, taking on enormous debt to help them out. Another young woman amassed credit card debt when she adopted her toddler niece from a drug-addicted sister. Another couple milked credit lines to adopt a baby.

Many people I have talked to see gift giving as central to debt. For some, their first charges were gifts. Popular magazines dwell on this allegedly out of control tendency at Christmas, urging readers to forego excessive gift-giving, to probe the possibly ill-conceived motives behind lavish gifts: Are you trying to make up for your own inadequate Christmases? Are you act-ing out of nostalgia, trying to re-create a Christmas you cannot really afford? Are you behaving childishly because Christmas evokes so many childhood memories? Are you "playing Santa" to too many? Why not purge your list? Cut people off? Or at least keep closer track of your purchases, use cash, or make your own presents? Others suggest a Christmas jar. Although these writers often make useful suggestions, they both illuminate and mask the myriad reasons Americans fall into debt.[16]

People have devised many ways to live with credit card debt. When they are broke, they may charge meals out with friends in order to collect cash. They must thus pay more in the form of interest, just as they once did when they had to charge food at drug stores and gourmet shops because grocery stores did not accept credit cards. In despair, people don't open the bills or stack them up and decide which ones they have to pay, often on the basis of how harshly they are being harassed. They send in a payment but don't sign the check. They don't answer the phone. One woman told *Glamour* magazine: "I used the last fifty dollars on my Visa card to buy an answering machine so I wouldn't have to answer calls from bill collectors."[17]

Some talk of cycles related to income interruptions: stockpiling cash and charging everything possible when in between jobs, paying down their balances when at work. "You're out of work, you charge as much as you can, trying to hoard cash. When you go back to work, you pay your cards down as much as you can, in preparation for the next time," explained a Washington freelancer. Others talk of credit card careers, slipping from one category to another, from convenience user to revolver because of an ill-timed crisis, then into lower and more expensive borrowing categories after involuntary unemployment, unexpected debt, a poorly insured accident, or a debilitating illness.

Revolvers *want* to pay off their credit card debt, as they demonstrated resoundingly in 1990 and, indeed whenever they have a surplus, they don't spend, they don't save, and they pay down debt.[18] For some, it is a life cycle issue, as they juggle the increased responsibilities of the middle years against their desire to gain control of their lives. One woman makes only minimum payments each month, with one bigger one, then calls and asks that bank to lower her credit limit to the difference. So if she owes $500, and pays $150, she asks them to lower her limit to $350. Friends and kin gather to cut up the cards of an excessive user or freeze their credit cards in ice cubes so that they have to think very hard about what they charge. Teresa Wilz describes the fate of her cards this way: "Deep freeze. As in literally and metaphorically. As in hanging out in the Frigidaire, encased in a Ziploc sandwich bag, nestled next to the ice cube tray, cuddling with a carton of Haagen-Dazs Mango Sorbet and a cryogenically preserved catfish filet."[19]

One man takes out a $6,000 cash advance to pay off all his other cards, making payments of $135/month, $130 of which is interest. Another man pays $100 a month, "gets back" $80 in credit, with the rest going to interest, and then heads to the grocery store for $75 worth of food. Debtors "use one to pay off the other" or "bounce our debt around from one company to the next." As one bumper sticker announces, "I use my MasterCard to pay my VISA."

The tabloid *Weekly World News* offered debtors ways to "get out of debt fast," which included patronizing bargain movies and consignment shops, insulating the attic, turning your hobby into extra income, putting all your spare change in a piggy bank every day, playing more card and board games, using the air dry setting on your dishwasher, and hiring yourself out as a handyman.[20]

Debtors try Debt Zapper programs and use the Credit Card Counseling service, where they turn themselves in and cut up their cards.

Hank Stuever interviewed credit card counselor Mary Rammel, "with her orange-handled scissors":

Rammel sees six or so clients a day, and they're always desperate. "They always ask me, 'Is this the worst debt you've ever seen?'" she says. "I always tell them I've seen worse. And I almost always have."

This morning it was a married couple in their eighties, with a fixed income of about $2,000 a month, a second mortgage and $62,000 in credit card debt. After hearing their story, and laying out a game plan for them, she took her scissors and cut up their cards, and put them in a large plastic jug where she collects the plastic—enough shards now to start a mosaic in a small basilica—Our Lady of Perpetual Indebtedness. She has filled four jugs. "At first I put them in this little candy jar," she says, pointing to a little glass jar on the windowsill.

Not infrequently, the people who seek Rammel's help are employed at the credit card banks.[21] Often this organization is able to negotiate longer term repayments from a fund it manages from issuers fearing absolute default. Secondary lenders through such programs as "Freedom Loan" offer the chance to consolidate debts under a new umbrella. And the Internet roils with the "Fresh Start" program and many other chances to fix bad credit. I received one in 1997, which read:

Dear Friend,

Are you or somebody that you know experiencing credit problems? If your answer is yes, I think you will be very interested in our special offer. No longer will you have to live like a second class citizen due to a bad credit report. Bad credit is caused by a variety of reasons: Health, divorce, and termination of employment, loss of income and dozens of other reasons. The bottom line is that bad credit can happen to anybody.

I could get a copy of my credit report and buy two manuals for a total of $94.00. In the summer of 2003, as I edited this book, I received four more. One read:

Hello brettwilliams.

We hope that your summer is off to a great start and your Independence Day was wonderful. Even though we are in the midst of summer, no doubt you have had lingering thoughts about the upcoming school year either for yourself or your children. In this week's article Kathleen Gurr goes over some of aspects of savings programs for college and is well worth the read. As the year progresses we also encourage to keep focused on your goal of becoming and staying debt free for life. It's easy to lose track of your resolutions while in the warm and carefree months of summer, but your goals are on the horizon, so keep them in your sights. Until next time, have a debt-free week. James Agnew Executive Vice President [22]

People also take on second jobs and put additional family members to work. In one case, a woman went to work outside the home solely to pay off credit card debt. They log more overtime, search for hidden expenses that often are not there, lower consumption, and write more checks. They hunt for bargains at thrift shops, yard sales, and discount grocery stores. They seek loans from relatives and increase pooling and sharing of rides, lawn mowers, child care and even credit cards.[23]

There are those who juggle their credit card balances, and banks reciprocate. One man described falling into debt over car repair and hardware bills, "joining MasterCard in 1988 to get out of hock to Sears" and because he wanted a "good printed record." He overcharged but got back within his limit. "I got it in order and stopped using my card for three months. They increased my credit limit, called me a good risk. Every time I did it we got a new line of credit."

Alternatively, some bankers now peek periodically at their customers' credit reports during the course of their relationship. If they fear a customer is becoming less creditworthy (for example, by racking up bills on other cards) they may raise their interest rates to penalty rates. When consumers started borrowing less, the banks flooded the market with tricky offers of "debt consolidation," a "low-interest starter loan" and "convenience checks." This aggressive marketing appealed largely to people who could not afford to carry more debt. Then, with their customers squeezed by the ever-higher interest rates allowed in the small print, the profits of banks' credit card operations soared. When a new law phased out tax deductions on credit card interest in 1986, a new marketing blitz aimed to capture home equity loans.

The problem is that marketing strategies do tempt us to be irresponsible, they do make it easier to spend what we do not have. Sweeteners such as discount coupons, special rates, or a 10 percent discount for first-time use may encourage greater consumption, socialize new users, and convince consumers that they are actually *more* fiscally responsible. The second card does come when your limit is up: in four months, one family received $53,000 worth of unsolicited credit. Another college graduate received more than $29,000 in credit following her one-year earnings of only $3,100. Comedian Tom Ryan notes the "potato chip-like quality"—can't just have one—of credit cards that swarm to a potential revolver: "I soon had purchasing power that would be the envy of many developing nations."[24]

Creditors are adept at trickery: flattering us with "preapproval," calling us "valued customers," "carefully selected from your community for a very special offer." Ryan points out that "pre-ruined" might be a better description of your state when a bank offers you a new card because you are maxed out, or raises your limit without your permission when you reach it (the debtor's reward for making minimum payments on time). Banks are also adept at making us feel slimy when once we were "valued" and special. Ryan notes that the addressee moves from being "Dear Mr. Ryan" to "Dear Borrower," and the dunning letter bears the look of "some kind of urgent telegram that was delivered to my mailbox by a bonded courier."[25] As Morrall writes in *Credit Card Management*, ". . . if the 30-day letter is a friendly reminder, the 60-day letter should express some concern."[26]

The banks kept searching for new ways to drum up more business. In 1986 Associates National Bank of California tried a test mailing to John Hancock Mutual Life policyholders: "This was a list of individuals that was relatively credit-saturated, notes Rebecca Young, vice president in charge of marketing for the banks. These cardholders also seem to ring up higher balances. So far, the average outstanding is 'significantly higher than for our own mailing program,' she reports."[27]

Bankers were also alert to new trends. In 1991, they observed that maxed-out citizens were finding it difficult to buy groceries and pay taxes, noted the increasing costs of health insurance, and scurried to capture that market. For example, *Credit Card Management*, an interesting name for an industry journal, noted that "rising health care costs may be the catalyst needed to make credit card acceptance among health care providers commonplace." In 1991, Visa and MasterCard pushed hard on supermarkets, knowing they were concerned about the recession. They urged these stores to accept credit cards to drive up sales, "maintain their customer base and give them insight into customer purchasing habits." And, one might add, to push shoppers entirely over the edge. That same year American Express headed for the Sears, K Mart, and Wal-Mart markets. *Chain Store Age Executive* urged banks to quickly harvest the great 1990s crop of new bankrupts, because they would not be able to refile for six years. And now the Church of God in Christ via Key Federal Bank issues affinity cards to help pay its expenses, even offering "secured cards" for those whose credit histories are "less than heavenly."[28]

Capital One epitomizes the ways that credit cards now work. Its developers saw a credit card as a formula composed of variables such as interest rate, credit line, and cash-advance line. Capital One issues thousands of cards, each slightly different and tailored to meet the different needs of people in terms of how they spend, borrow, and procrastinate. It pioneered balance-transfer offers and the teaser rate. The company slashed interest for the best borrowers and devised "appropriate" rates for the worst. It has tinkered with credit lines, mileage awards, design of the cards, even the color of the envelopes. It knows when to invite you to skip a payment or when to change the grace period and may lower your credit line if you pay late and then charge you an over the limit fee. It may raise your interest rate if you carry a high balance and stop charging. Capital One has jacked up the annual percentage rate to 24.3 percent for customers piling up too much debt with other companies. Your account may be canceled if you don't charge enough or if you pay too fully and faithfully. The company has pursued different ways of retaining customers and pursuing malingerers, targeting smaller and smaller segments from its huge data base, so that as consumers we almost literally embody credit and debt. Nonbank Providian, another shady lender, *requires* that cardholders limit the total they charge on other cards. If they do not, Providian can cancel with the entire balance due immediately. Or Providian may close your account if you never carry a balance and pay interest.[29]

How does it end? We hope that a relative might die or that we'll hit the lottery or have a good year. Realtors hope for an especially good commission. Some people hope to win on a game show.

"Debt," once a hit show on the Lifetime cable channel, pays the debt of the contestant who most successfully answers questions concerning popular culture trivia. They begin each day with a negative total that reflects their total debt, up to $10,000. Whoever whittles away the most debt proceeds to a speed round of questions. If you answer ten you get a check equivalent to the rest of your debt, again capped at $10,000. Then winners face a final temptation: they can wager all their money, to double it or go home empty. The loser gets a plastic piggy bank and a $500 savings bond.

Contestants faced a long wait to get on the show. They were most likely to be chosen if they were young—20s, 30s, 40s—and could tell a compelling tale: a stock crash, a pregnancy, or a yearlong tour with the Grateful Dead. "People like to hear other people talk about money the same way that they like to hear them talk about sex," said Dr. David W. Krueger, a Houston psychoanalyst. "Either they get a feeling of connection—'Good. Someone else has a lot of debt, too'—or they feel superior. Either way, it's a good feeling for the viewer."[30]

Imagining Debt

In the face of this rude exploitation of problems *they* caused, why aren't we angry at banks? Why instead do we blame debtors? Why is it so easy to seize on such exotica as the revolver's upside-down conceptualization "My balance is my savings"? How can we laugh at people like the young woman who showed me a drawer full of cards and explained "These don't work anymore"? Why do we cling to noxious stereotypes comparing debt to drug addiction, even when we're talking about ourselves? One woman told me, "For the first time I had a charge-free Christmas. It was like coming away from drug abuse." And a man said of his wife, "She was trying to fill a void, and I was a pleaser." Indeed, talk of codependency and enabling fill the popular literature on credit cards. Reporter Warsh writes, "There is something especially pernicious about bank-card revolving credit, which exploits people's shortsightedness to consume now and pay later. . . . The bankers were defeating the purposes of the CRA [Community Reinvestment Act], not through redlining, but by hooking relatively low-income consumers on streams of highly profitable consumer credit. . . . Like cigarettes, drugs, and gambling, they are engines of addiction. Throughout, bankers have been leading the borrowing binge."[31]

In *Parade* magazine, Andrew Tobias echoed this philosophy:

Make up your mind to break the habit. Your life is 20 percent more expensive than it needs to be. The banks love you. You lend them money via your deposits at 5 percent or less, and borrow it back at 18 percent or more. Look yourself in the eye and just make up your mind to do it. Cut up your credit cards. Boiling doesn't work—it remained unfazed—just floating around, winking its hologram at me. Withdraw money from your savings account. Hold a yard sale. Skip store-bought gifts this holiday season.[32]

Margaret Talbot laments the destructive and predictable character of this "narrative arc" purporting to describe America's addiction to credit.

She argues that the arc moves through temptation and a downward spiral until the debtor hits rock bottom. Then "the language of addiction and recovery kicks in." Thus we point the finger at lack of financial stability instead of inequality. The addiction story—debt porn—lends middle- and upper-class consumers a "smug sense of maturity and responsibility."[33]

Often these stereotypes are gendered. One man talked at length of "the little secretaries pretending to make more than they do." The compulsively shopping, bored housewife is a well-worn vacuous figure of fun. Many men spoke to me of their ex-wives' debt. As one man put it, "I was married, but now I'm divorced and the proud owner of a credit card bill that will cost me one paycheck a month for the next two years." Another man spoke of his wife's debt: "I'm a living proof of the problems. My wife has had to have $30,000 worth of therapy. I feel a lot of anger and resentment working full-time to pay her debt off. There were things I didn't know were there, couldn't identify. Consuming made her feel better. It was money in her pocket. You feel betrayed, like she cheated on you."

Newspapers sometimes helped to fuel both the addiction and gender stereotypes. The *Chicago Tribune* devoted an article to women's out-of-control shopping, which they had to conceal from their husbands. One woman said that she spent money on the kids when she really bought a new outfit. Another saved plastic dry cleaning bags and says she just picked up the dry cleaning. Another "paid" the utility bills twice a month, keeping one payment for herself. Another smuggled new clothes in her briefcase. In the worst case, a woman could not get off a month-long shopping binge and spent $90,000 on clothes, furs, and jewelry. When her husband put a hold on her cards she pawned her purchases to buy some more. The article continues with flighty anecdotes of women who hide their credit card bills (with the help of a female postal carrier) and disguise their new purchases in thrift store bags, thwarting the noble efforts of their husbands to put a hold on their cards or cut them up. A Los Angeles teacher claims, "Men just don't understand that shopping is our drug of choice."[34]

On the other hand, Vince Passaro writes of his long-suffering wife:

This kind of stripping of the family accounts needed spousal consultation. When I told my wife the news she was surprisingly understanding, for a woman who'd been urging me for two years to go and see a judge and work out some kind of deal on the parking tickets; for a woman whose husband's car had been towed for tickets twice before (that is, for a woman whose husband rather adamantly makes the same mistakes twice, or three times); for a woman whose rent and grocery money was about to go through a scratched Plexiglas window to get back a ten-year-old car with 122,000 miles on it, only two (of four) working power windows, and $600 still to pay on the loan we'd taken to purchase it.[35]

Sometimes these stereotypes express generational concerns. Katherine Newman points out that many baby boomer parents feel that their adult children "could make a down payment if only they didn't eat out so much." The baby boomers blame themselves at the same time their parents blame *themselves* for how they raised them. This "self-critical, intergenerational judging" does not illuminate the situation, nor does the silly mythology surrounding allegedly atavistic yuppies.[36] Credit cards have helped to create an artificial middle class, disguising their declining fortunes. At the same time, the debt bankcards generate is so confusing that we cannot see the real beneficiaries of it; we rail about class (when we do it at all), at the poor, or at some kind of political class, rather than at big business.

Debt implies dependency, being incomplete, hanging like a pendant. Islam forbids usury, and in the Bible debt is everywhere as a stand-in for sin. Shakespeare wrote, "Neither a borrower nor a lender be." Debt can also speak to an *inter*dependency that recognizes the vagaries, difficulties, shifting needs, obligations and relations of social life. The debt of a sharecropper, an immigrant, a miner, a trader, or a religious devotee expresses and enacts relations of unequal power, the ebb and flow of resources, promises and commitments over time. But as modern American debtors struggle to preserve their dignity, keep up appearances, and posit that they're middle class, they feel guilty, complicit, and conflicted, as though credit card companies are their (perhaps untrustworthy) friends. The woman who financed her children's college education using credit cards, argued, "I was lucky to have them." Many use metaphors of falling, which naturalize debt and de-emphasize human agency: "It was a sinking ship" or "I was deep in the ditch."[37] Or sometimes we talk about mountains of debt. We chip or whittle away at it, or pare it down. One woman said, "It's like a dark cloud hanging over you all the time. It just creeps into every aspect of your life.[38] Passaro writes of a

credit card treadmill. . . . Right now, we're averaging 20 percent annual interest, so the interest alone, compounding and compounding, like a fracture, is around $475 per month. . . . We have to earn $8500 a year just to service our credit-card debt, never mind pay it back. The consumer credit-card debt comes to more than $28,000 overall, the interest rolling on, like Woodie Guthrie's Columbia River.[39]

We feel ashamed and isolated, as though debt were a perfectly private affair. The pretense nags at us.

As one man put it, "I was just trying to live like a grownup." Another woman told *Glamour*: "I realized there was something wrong when I was paying 19 percent interest on my Visa card while my teeth were rotting."[40]

The political consequences are tragic. Credit cards mask exorbitant prices, ease unfair transactions, and may undermine unions by disguising our falling wages. We take more abuse because they help us through hard times. One woman tolerated car payments of $300 a month on a non-working Mercury Sable because she could make the expensive repair bills on credit. She also failed to pursue action against the dealership or the company until she was maxed out. She then skipped several car payments in protest. She still suffers from bad credit because she was belatedly berating the company about her ill-made car.

"We are so choked by a collar of debt," lamented another debtor, "that it makes us selfish." "Who inherits my father's credit card debt when he dies?" one woman wrote in *Woman's Day*.[41] A California resident speculates that anti-immigrant sentiment undergirding Proposition 209 may stem from the perception of a culture suffering from strangling, vexing debt. Could the virulent attacks on the black poor stem in part from middle-class consternation about debt? Why can we not see the unproductive uses to which credit card companies are putting our money, sucking it away from opportunities for investment, home ownership, or interesting work?

A gulf of practice and meaning splits convenience users and megacharg-ers from revolvers. To many convenience users free credit has come to seem as much of an entitlement as the mortgage interest deduction. Some feel self-righteous about it, as though those who pay interest are misguided, greedy, vain, or foolish. Some feel the horror and disbelief expressed by a woman in Texas who was shocked that her friend, a schoolteacher, died leaving a balance on her Visa. They sometimes feel surprised and angry when I suggest that poorer people are subsidizing their free credit. Many feel dismayed and complicit, because they had no idea that their free credit can only exist as long as poorer people pay a much higher interest rate. Some are startled to discover how bankers characterize them. "Me! A dead-beat?" exclaimed one longtime careful cardholder from Massachusetts. Pay-ing a credit card bill feels like paying a utility bill: it does not *seem* like free credit. As one convenience user noted, "It looks the same. You pay your bills for the expenses you incurred last month. It might feel different if they made you a loan at the *beginning* of the month. It's hard to figure out."[42]

Why Is This All So Hard to Understand?

Our culture has responded to its sharp division between haves and have-nots by making money into a dream, a private religious experience, an unspeakable ecstasy or a wordless horror. A great deal of shame surrounds money—for those who have lots of it, those who have little, and those who are uncomfortably stationed in be-tween. I know much more about my friends' sex lives than I do about their finances.

I know about their polyps, the lumps that tested negative, the growths and stones and reflux and misshaped toe bones . . . I know whether they're on 20 mg or 40 mg of Prozac or that they've made the switch to Zoloft; I know the very bad things their parents did to them. The one thing they will never permit to be known about them, to any friend, the only thing that cannot be discussed, is how much money they have in the bank. . . . Therefore, we have no joint knowledge of how we are dealing with the money issues in our lives; each of us faces the problem alone.[43]

The Language of Debt

One way to bridge this moral divide is to understand that the banking industry promoted images and metaphors obscuring debt, pretending that most credit card use is convenience use, at the very time that it was seeking customers who would be most likely to revolve. The contrast between what bankers said and what they did jarred many of us with a gap between lived experience and dominant cultural meanings.[44] On the other hand, their portrayal of credit cards as benign, helpful companions appeared to match the experiences and perceptions of more advantaged customers. This section examines more closely the cloudy metaphors that permeated industry talk, the misleading language of credit card advertising, and the twisted thrust of various political campaigns that offered regressive solutions to the debt crisis and framed those solutions to make conditions appear the opposite of what they were.

Throughout this chapter I have alluded to the language shrouding credit card activities: a preferred customer, bowed with debt but slowly, faithfully paying it off holds a "mature account." The add-on fees of 3–4 percent that merchants must pay Visa and MasterCard, which they pass on to us as increased prices, are called "discount fees." "Debt capacity" refers to the maximum amount of debt a person can be burdened with, and to "saturate" it means that a bank has succeeded in doing so. The statement "Revolvers pay the float for nonrevolvers" appears to describe impartially a financial system where poorer people who must pay interest subsidize free credit for the more affluent.

The linguistic quagmire into which we have sunk over the last twenty years is thick indeed. Everything is backwards, mirroring the out-of-synch economy where there seems to be no relationship between what we earn and what we do and have. Money seems irrelevant: it's all debt. A reversal of meaning accompanies our reversal of fortune: to accumulate a balance means the opposite of what it used to mean.

When communicating to each other, bankers use metaphors of war and water: beachhead, penetration, saturation, float, debt capacity, and target. People are consumers. When lobbying or testifying to Congress their language becomes proprietary and technocratic, as they speak of pricing, supply, caps, spread, stickiness, financial services, and *citizens*. As they solicit our business, we become valued, preapproved, preferred, creditworthy, select customers, or *members*, "worthy" of relationship banking, affinity cards, and grace, in timeworn metaphors from domestic and religious life. We make choices, we are disciplined with penalties, but we can usually have a second chance. Mass marketing boosts the values of freedom and mastery: "Master the moment", "It's everywhere you want to be", "Membership has its privileges", "The Freedom Card". "It pays to Discover, you deserve it . . . Why wait?" "Have it the way you want it with Visa." The popular press counters with mocking scofflaw terms stemming from the worlds of hunting, fishing, dancing, and sex: trolling, surfing, poaching, dunning, teaser, sweetener, and shuffle. How are we ever to understand what is really going on?

Moreover, industry language pretends that credit card users act out of personal choice and convenience. Charlene Sullivan of the Credit Research Center writes, "One of the principal benefits of the credit card, from the cardholder's point of view, is that the cardholder controls the timing of his or her use of credit up to the specified credit limit"[45] Federal Reserve Board Governor Seger argues to Congress that Americans like credit cards because "the terms of repayment are flexible and at the discretion of the holder . . . Credit card debt has expanded rapidly for two years [1983–85] . . . a sign that consumers view credit card uses as a desirable source of short-term financing despite what many observers regard as high rates of interest."[46]

The distortions of industry trade talk are matched by advertisers' themes that pretend that all credit card use is convenience use. Names like C. F. Frost, Joan Young, and Thomas Hill dot ads like "Membership has its privileges," which the American Express campaign launched in 1987. Visa countered with "Membership has its disadvantages," a campaign including a map of Madrid featuring 1,000 places accepting Visa, and only one taking American Express, as though most credit card holders used them to travel! In 1985, Chase Visa World Card used a TV spot positioning the card as a financial planning tool for an upscale audience: "For those who are accustomed to having options, we offer many . . . the option to go . . . the option to see . . . the option to do . . . and just when you think you've exercised all your options, you appreciate that you have one more very attractive option—the World Card allows you to spread your payments. To use the card as a financial tool. To control your money."

Playing with words such as *options, freedom,* and *control,* implying power, this advertisement was not unique in concluding: "Enjoy the freedom you've earned . . . to travel . . . to entertain . . . to spend." These ads spun a carefully woven web to first entice and then entrap revolvers, not the convenience users they pretended to want to attract.

The business pages of newspapers have often discerned important trends in the marketing and use of credit cards. But reporters have not often linked the proliferation of credit cards to a distressed economy, or to conscious banking strategies, abetted by government research, subsidies, and regulatory policies, to trap people in debt. Too often the business pages treat credit cards as a topic in their own right, separate from other political and economic processes. Popular writers overlook revolvers' circumstances, or else take this gulf for granted. For example, financial analysts Albert Crenshaw and Jerry Knight perhaps assumed that their readers lived on one side of the abyss when they wrote: "But if you carry a $10,000 balance, and *believe (it) or not, thousands of people do*—interest would cost you $1540 a year on a 15.4 percent card and $1200 on a 12 percent card."[47]

The smoke and mirrors seeping through commercials, industry position statements, and the mainstream press make it hard to get a grasp on the whole system. Debt does not allow us to "Master the moment" or "Be everywhere we want to be," but drains resources, drags us and our future down, propels inequality, and masks race, class, gender, and generational differences while exacerbating tensions, divisions, and inequities that run along precisely those axes.

Usury Comes Back

This twisting of the story is especially clear (or unclear) in the debate about usury ceilings, why they were unnecessary, and how dire would be the repercussions that would follow them. This debate emerged in 1985, 1986, and again in 1991, thanks in part to the tenacity of Senator D'Amato from New York, who persisted in introducing bills to cap interest rates.[48] The problem was that no matter how low other interest rates dropped, credit card rates stayed high, or sticky, a "regular honey pot," financial reporter Warsh appropriately termed them.[49] To call credit card rates "sticky" is to naturalize these rates, as though no human actions are responsible for their staying high, while banks refused to cut profits at all in the face of soaring personal debt. Credit card interest seemed to defy the economic forces of gravity, and in fact edged upward toward 19 percent. Congress considered several possibilities: that caps should be a flat 14 percent, or not more than 5 percent above the discount rate, or no more than 6 percent above the yield on three-month treasury notes. Each time the Federal Reserve Board took its opposition to the floor: " 'The board . . . has endorsed the principle that consumer loans and other types of credit are most fairly and efficiently allocated when there are no regulatory constraints on interest rates. Indeed, the Board has been concerned for some time about the adverse impact that rate ceilings can have on the availability of funds in local credit markets,' explained FRB Governor Seger in 1985."[50]

The poison of deregulation, argued the Federal Reserve Board, would seep through the economy, with multiplier effects. First, lower interest ceilings would cause a sharp contraction in consumer spending, because customers would rebel against the devices banks would invent to recoup their lost interest. The most vulnerable banks would fail. Then bankers would probably withdraw *all* credit, devastating less affluent borrowers. Thus the middle class would be punished for the actions of parasitic revolvers, whom Seger blamed for high interest rates in a skillful twist of reality: "As a result of Americans who obtain credit but cannot pay off their debts, middle-class America pays, and they pay in the form of higher interest rates. The rich do not pay because they pay off their monthly bills in full."[51]

Rejecting usury ceilings in favor of a more timid and regressive path, Congress passed the Tax Reform Act of 1986, which phased out the deductibility of interest paid on credit cards, but not the sacrosanct mortgage or home equity loan and not interest incurred from leveraged buyouts. This shield had lowered the cost of credit for the falling middle class suffering from the economic dislocations of the 1980s. However, its critics argued that the deduction had been regressive in rewarding only those borrowers who also itemized. This argument is true, but it is also disingenuous, for the new tax law certainly hurt revolvers more than convenience users, who paid no interest anyway. It taxed small borrowers but not the deal makers who mobilized million-dollar loans for takeover campaigns. It taxed renters' interest but not that of homeowners, to whom banks immediately reached out with a home equity loan campaign.[52]

Bankers thought that usury ceilings had disappeared in 1986. But the problem returned to haunt them in 1991 at a fund-raising dinner where President Bush praised the steadfast Senator D'Amato for his relentless assault on high interest rates. Wasting no time, D'Amato introduced a flat 14 percent usury cap bill the next day. It rolled through the Senate in thirty minutes and headed for the House.

Bankers protested with furious faxes, spirited lobbying, and full-page newspaper advertisements, in which credit suddenly became the civil right they had contested in 1974. "Will Congress Deny Millions of Americans the Right to Keep Their Credit Cards? Potentially, up to half of those citizens currently holding credit cards would no longer qualify," railed the American Bankers Association.[53] Note that all of a sudden we were citizens, rather than consumers. Popular writers echoed this theme of the credit card as a fundamental civil right, ensuring proper identification, a package of consumer services, and assistance in emergencies. The Dow Jones dropped

120 points, and Bush administration officials hit the talk-show circuit to backpedal. Treasury Secretary Nicholas Brady termed the caps "wacky, senseless," on "Meet the Press": "The only people who would have credit cards would be the rich people." The bill would "lead to credit cards which are elitist." "The key here is for consumers to shop around," reiterated Lawrence B. Lindsey, also from the Federal Reserve Board of Governors. Even Senator D'Amato was finally reined in, although he still criticized the banks:

"Maybe credit should not be so readily available. We do not do people a service by failing, sufficiently, to check out their background, but letting them run up the tab and saying, well, we have the rest of working middle-class Americans who are going to pick up the tab by paying extra credit. They ought to be a little more careful as to what kind of people they give credit cards to."

But he went on to say: "Banks have got a captive audience, particularly given the present state of the economy. Consumers are so happy to have a source of credit, any source of credit that they pay up and shut up. I think that is wrong. Banks should not be allowed to take advantage of consumers' need for credit. Banks argue that credit card operations are their only source of profit these days. Why should consumers bear the burden of being the profit source for large, money-hungry banks?[54]

Senator D'Amato made two significant points: that some citizens are irresponsible and that banks are money-hungry. Only his first theme filtered through a popular culture already attuned to "We are all careful convenience users here" mythology. For example, in a letter published in *Newsday*, Mayo Gottliebson complained:

28 percent operating costs for collections! The middle-income group is paying for purchases made by these non-creditworthy individuals by means of usurious finance charges that are imposed by the banks. The banks claim that if the finance charge rate were reduced to 14 percent they would have to withdraw millions of credit cards. . . . This, they contend, would be disastrous to the economy. In other words, the banks are saying that the middle-income group should continue to pay for purchases made by deadbeats so as not to disturb the national economy. What kind of reasoning is that?"[55]

Like Madeline Smith, Gottliebson does not realize that *he* is the one bankers might consider a deadbeat!

Successful in the usury fight, bankers still had to grapple with heavily burdened debtors by 1990. They tried to steal each other's customers through the balance transfer wars and to hold on to their own by increasing the credit limits of the "best" customers in their portfolios. In 1995 card companies mailed out more than 2.4 billion unsolicited credit offers.[56] This siege reflected the fierce, new competition in the industry, driven in part by bank deregulation, which allowed nonbanks to act like banks and encouraged them all to find more ways to make money. Some of the largest credit card issuers in 1996 were banks in name only, like First USA, with 12 million cards in circulation, and AT&T Universal Bank, with 23 million cards.

Since 1993 the national total for revolving credit has climbed at an annualized rate nearing 20 percent, three times the rate of personal-income growth. In 1995 we paid $65 billion in interest, more than the gross national product of Egypt at $50 billion. Since 1994 late fees and other penalty fees have supplemented interest in keeping the industry floating in profit. In 2000 customers paid $6.6 billion in penalty fees.[57]

In 1996 household debt totaled 89 percent of annual disposable income. By 1996 credit card delinquencies were at 3.96 percent, their highest level since 1981, and a "new breed" of well-salaried, low-risk debtors were making news by filing for bankruptcy.[58] In 1996, 1.2 million people filed for bankruptcy, a whopping 22 percent increase from the year before. By 2001 the average person filing for bankruptcy had a net income of $21,444, total expenses of $24,324, and a total debt of $82,852.[59] Others had been able to take advantage of home equity loans by borrowing against the amount they had paid off on their mortgages. By 1997 home equity debt totaled $170 billion, up 68 percent from 1990. By the end of 2000 consumer debt was growing at a rate of 12 percent a year, versus 5.5 percent a year in 1998, but at the same time home equity debt was continuing to grow, tripling in terms of number of people. The rise in both types of debt signals distress, for people often refinance their mortgage to pay off other debts.[60]

More and more, revolvers are us. But the financial services industry has long moved on to explore another frontier.

Chapter 4
Seducing Students

Sometime in the early 1990s I began to notice something new. When students arrived at my university to begin classes, a host of credit card advertisements welcomed them back. These ads beamed from bulletin boards, peered out of shopping bags, lurked on tables near the advising offices, and peppered radio and television. On the quad young salespeople persuaded students to apply for credit cards by offering them free Skittles, Tootsie Rolls, M & M's, baby boom boxes, dictionaries, mugs, baseball caps, water bottles, sunglasses, airline vouchers, and such T-shirts as "Daytona, MasterCard," promising a fun-filled spring break. In a full-page advertisement in our student newspaper, Discover Card warned: "Those Who Can, Do. (Those who can't sit in their dorm and eat macaroni and cheese) If you don't got it, get it."[1]

"MasterCard International . . . So Worldly. So Welcome" offered romantic cruises, grand spectacles, exotic shows, and white, sandy beaches. Jerry Seinfeld, abandoned on a desert island, hopped to safety on a cruise ship because he had his American Express card. "Run with it . . . Fly with it/Life's an adventure," proclaimed American Express. In the "*Unofficial Student Guide*," AmEx announced, "A couple of students talk frankly about their lives, their hopes, and how to save serious money on airline tickets." One of these students plans a trip to the beach to "study her major." Discover drew on educational analogies (sort of) to claim, "You can't judge a book by its cover . . . if you don't have the book." Or better yet, "Life's a book. Skip to the good parts," backgrounded by its orange and black card with a bright sun (the future?) shining through the O. Visa offered the less reassuring message "Visa: accepted at more places than you were."

Many advertisements promoted causes: through PlanetCard, you can "use this card to be a credit to Planet Earth!" Or you can feel proud knowing that a percentage of profits will fund a "Citi Student Center." In 1994 Citibank hired a disabled man to persuade students to sign up so that "his organization would receive a profit." Citi also hired young "contracts" to organize sorority and fraternity keg parties, where the club received $1.00

for each signed application and \$2.50–\$3.00 for each one that was mailed in.[2]

Faculty all got letters from Chase Manhattan Bank. Chase "would like to help your students get the credit they deserve. . . . Please make this offer available to your students by placing the enclosed applications in the holder on a bulletin board in a high traffic area or display them with other take-one information in your offices." I hope we didn't do it. Even if we were unaware in the early 1990s of how badly creditors were bilking our students, we were appalled by their mockery of a college education. And their massacre of the language gave me chills. Students who were learning to think and write were being bombarded with stupid puns about credit, misspellings, made-up words, bad grammar, and ugly cliches. If they wished, they could learn from these solicitations how to lie. My spellchecker can hardly hack through them.

In 1994, anthropologist Kelly Andrews collected solicitations from around our quad and noted the pernicious themes that linked credit card holding to adulthood and autonomy. From American Express: "Get the Card That Puts You in Control / It's Your Life. Take Charge of it." Discover reminded students, "You Were Born Free. . . . So Why Pay to Live? Isn't it time you applied, yourself?" Find emancipation from meddlesome parents: "Enjoy the Freedom and Flexibility of a Bank-One Visa or MasterCard. . . . No need to have a parent or guardian co-sign your application." Visa went even further, linking credit cards to the rights of citizenship, akin to voting, entering into contracts, and serving in the armed forces.[3] Solicitations never shut up about adulthood, citizenship, and maturity, although behind the scenes one market researcher referred to the whole thing as a "training-wheels operation."[4] The contradictions were ridiculous, the marketing duplicitous. Credit card issuers admitted to each other or when pressed by reporters that they knew parents would bail their kids out. And when parents could, they did. Albert Crenshaw cites youth marketer Durant Abernathy, who noted that one of his own daughters got into trouble: "You could say I got burned. . . . But at least she learned in the process. . . . College is a time to learn, to make the transition to adulthood."[5]

Credit card solicitations also promised students the opportunity to build a credit history to ensure themselves a secure future. "Get the Card and get ready for take-off"; "It's a smart decision to start building a good credit history to get those important loans you'll need later / Let BankOne help you get started on your future." "Forecasting a Bright Financial Future / Whether you're a fiery Aries or a romantic Libra, enhance your future with a Visa or MasterCard with your Astrological Sign" from 1st Financial Bank. From BankAmericard: "Credit Earned . . . Credit Due . . . A strong beginning to your financial independence."

At the same time, card companies appeared altruistic and concerned. They seemed to promise that they would replace families by keeping students safe. "Count on Citibank to be there for you", "Rely on Citibank, anytime, anywhere. . . . We want to make being out on your own a little easier." "More help making ends meet/We're there for you. No matter when, no matter what," crooned American Express. Perhaps the most egregious example, although it's difficult to choose, was the Citibank promise to give students "feelings of safety, security, and general wellness not unlike those experienced in the womb. Therefore [Citibank Classic Visa card] is the mother of all credit cards."[6]

The marketing that met students when they arrived at school ridiculed a university education. Credit card advertisements distorted ideas of freedom, adulthood, merit, autonomy, loyalty, and social concern. They offered to replace families and teachers in giving care, guidance, consolation, and fun; they mocked students' academic majors, #2 pencils, literacy, books, deadlines, membership, and civic engagement. They taunted students with power.

Today these solicitations appear more restrained—as well they might, given the outrage the early marketers provoked. In 2002 Chase Platinum urged, "Achieve your next milestone with Chase Platinum for Students." AT&T Universal Platinum MasterCard oozes, "You've got personality. This card does, too. This card is so YOU. Whatever your quirks, we've got the perks. . . . But with freedom comes responsibility. . . . So make your payments on time. Do not exceed your credit limit. And keep us informed if you need assistance."

So they've finally shut up about adulthood and citizenship. But what you can barely, if ever, decipher are the truly hideous terms. It took me two days, on and off, and a lot of help to figure this out from the Chase Platinum brochure, but I think I'm right. It was hard to imagine being eighteen, new to college and having the time, the mistrust, or the doggedness to decipher it all. The introductory interest rate of 2.9 percent lures you in. The preferred interest rate of 15.99 percent is reserved for customers who never pay late or miss a payment to this company *or any other creditor*. (They use their database to peek into your life every month to ascertain how you're doing.) The default interest rate (of *at least* 22.99 percent) punishes and flattens those customers who mess up. These rates, however, are variable, tied to the prime (the rate that banks pay their wealthiest customers), so they go up and down unpredictably. (What remains predictable is the profit to the lender.) In addition, if you carry a balance, you pay interest on interest. For example, if you only make a minimum payment the first month, the interest you owed on the original purchase becomes part of the new balance. If you are late or bounce a check or go over your limit, you pay fines, which also become part of the original money you borrowed. So you also pay interest on the penalty fees! There's also a 50 cent transaction fee on every charge. If you're a typical cash-poor student, you make minimum payments to all your creditors absolutely faithfully every month, you pay interest on interest, and you carry credit card debt forever. You're stuck, schmuck. (If all this math is daunting, you can go straight to the cash advance fee or the annual percentage rate charged for cash advances. In December 2003, my niece, a student at Brown, paid a fee of $30 for a cash advance of $100, which she will repay at an APR of 362.77%. I think—even these figures are hard to figure.)

Customers for Life

Are students learning to be thoughtful and informed citizens, hedonistic consumers, or thoroughly defeated debtors for life? Why did the credit card companies come to campus? To answer this question, I return to the mid-1980s to retrace the steps that led to the convocation of debt that welcomes students to campus each year.

College credit card promotions appear slick and facile, but the financial services industry needed to be cagey, imaginative, and persistent to bully their way into this new market. Some sensed trouble by 1985 with their increasingly debt-saturated revolvers. In noxious natural imagery, "banks had found a lush oasis in credit cards" and "blanketed the country," but "too much tilling threatens to deplete this once-fertile soil."[7] Issuers had solicited and resolicited to the point of exhaustion, yet response and activation rates seemed stuck. Where could credit card issuers go from here?

There are still a few markets where the bank credit card has not penetrated deeply. College students, for example, have been largely unpursued, except by the giant card issuers, namely Citicorp and American Express. And there are 12 million of them, with an estimated disposable income of some $40 billion annually—a proverbial gold mine for the astute marketer.[8]

A shrewd Citibank official commented that "well-structured credit programs for teenagers" can bring in high profits. *Glamour* magazine weighed in, arguing that college students do need credit cards and offering tips for getting started: hitch a ride on your parents' card, start with a store or gasoline card, consider a collateralized account.[9]

"Penetration" moved slowly at first. In 1986, college students stubbornly persisted in writing checks, using them nine times as often as they charged. Bankers once again pursued research that might reveal to them the complexities and contradictions of this target group. Students' needs and wants received ponderous marketing attention.[10]

Researchers found that students would respond to approaches targeted directly at them. Students appeared particularly interested in the environment and in good health. They read more than most Americans and therefore tuned in to relatively inexpensive print media. Campus life was more difficult than it used to be, students faced grim job prospects, and they knew it, so they might respond to solicitations in unpredictable ways.[11]

Further, industry analysts argued, the college market encompassed both a teenage and an adult market, a current and future source of profits. Students found it fast and easy to acquire several cards and max them out. But students were worth the risk because their parents often bailed them out of trouble. Moreover, customers tended to develop brand loyalties between the ages of eighteen and twenty-four. Hook them young, and they will be faithful, lasting customers. Visa's research showed that three out of four college students kept their first credit card for fifteen years or more. Also, "every year, a new crop comes into the fold." (So now they're lambs?) Banks patient enough to wrestle with students' complexities and contradictions could harvest "customers for life."[12]

Credit card companies were resourceful and inventive in seducing students. In 1988, Visa sponsored the Olympic Games, inspiring MasterCard to host World Cup soccer in 1994. Visa donated $1,000 to the athletic departments of every college that appeared on CBS in the fall of 1989 as well as $1,000 to the U.S. Olympic Team.

In the early 1990s, Citibank was one of the most aggressive suitors, offering a Student Citi Package, with checking, saving, overdraft protection, and a credit card. AT&T offered students, whom they called the "13 million independents," a three-in-one, free-for-life Universal card, including a bank card, credit card, and telephone calling card. MasterCard's Master-Values program extended a mix of discounts, financial seminars, concerts, and scholarship competitions. They followed students to spring break in Florida, offering a free T-shirt for each completed application. MasterCard also sponsored a College Music Tour of alternative rock bands in 1993–94, signing up customers along the way, giving out 25,000 free CDs, one with each completed application.[13]

Since 1989, "kiddie card" ownership has soared, reflecting both the increasing financial pressures on college students as well as the ease in qualifying for credit cards. A 1991 survey showed that 49 percent of students had four or more credit cards, and only 18 percent paid off their balances each month.[14] By 1995, 42 percent of Americans between eighteen and twenty-four, and 75 percent of full-time undergraduates, held credit cards. According to industry estimates, issuers earned $16.5 million a year on every 100,000 student cardholders. More than $10 million of this was interest income.[15]

In response to college resistance and some citizen outrage, banks initiated "financial literacy" programs. Citi introduced Max Moore, Detective in Moneytown, who used comedy to "aid students in financial distress and guide them back to the road to financial success." A variety of scenarios featured "The Case of the Fumblin' Frosh," "The Case of the Creeping Balance," and "The Case of the Maxin' Out Kid" (which reminds students not to have too many credit cards). MasterCard developed a personal finance video and teachers' guide called "MasterYour Future," a college seminar called "Mastering Your Money," and a magazine titled *College FundAmentals*.[16] Visa issued a booklet, "Credit Cards: An Owners Manual," in 1991, which starred the cartoon character Cathy. The story begins as she asks, "First Love: Am I unworthy? First credit card: I am worthy!" The plot follows Cathy through giddy, girlish misadventures like a shopping spree for shoes, then happily marries her off at the end. Presumably, her wise and prudent husband will retire her credit card debt.

The ever more intense competition also drove credit card issuers into high schools to offer financial education supplements to thousands of students and teachers. "It used to be that college was the big free-for-all for new customers," Marian Saltzman, president of a youth marketing firm, told the *New York Times*. "But now, the big push is to get them between 16 and 18." Discover published "Starting Earlier" (with interactive video "educational" programs about personal finance) and attached its "Extra-Credit" supplement to *Scholastic* magazine. The final page featured students in a classroom backgrounded by a huge Discover card and urged, "Go ahead, we're behind you!" Visa offered "Choices and Decisions," a twelve-chapter, multimedia financial-literacy curriculum for fifteen- to eighteen-year-olds, which it sold to member banks and donated to local schools.

Why high school, because outside of 90210 most high school students can't possibly represent much money? "We are trying to make kids more financially responsible," argued Beth Metzler, Vice President of Discover. "To make Discover as legitimate as Visa and MasterCard." Metzler pointed out that high school students don't know the difference between cards, and issuers "aren't willing to take the chance that a competitor can establish an early beachhead." "It's an act of faith . . . a bridge between Discover and the thought processes that will happen when these kids need to establish credit," she explained.[17] In 1992, 640,000 high school students carried credit cards. "Within five years, your typical 15-year old will have at least a $300 credit limit on a major card," predicted a New York youth marketer.

In 1997, my sixteen-year-old son, an unemployed, debt-financed soccer player, was offered a soccer affinity card.

They knew what they were doing, and they did it on purpose.

A Spoiled Journey

In 1994, Visa sued Radford University student Michelle Bedell for a debt of $1,481. Bedell countersued. She argued that Visa had taken advantage of her inexperience and naivete to load her down with debt, and that she should not have to pay the interest she had accrued at a rate of 23.8 percent, so that her purchases of $838 had ballooned into a bill of $1,481.00. Later, testifying before Congress, Bedell described slipping into credit card debt and maintained:

after months of talk and random payments, I found myself with ruined credit and warrant-in-debt for the balance of the VISA account. And that's when I decided that I would stop payments on the card because I wasn't paying any money that would help my status as a credit applicant in the future. I mean, it was just—it seemed like a waste to me to keep paying when I was—my credit was already ruined. . . . Basically, I just, I mean, I tried to do the right thing. And now I am kind of in a hole.

Her mother Connie Bedell argued,

My [twin] children, in their senior year, have not used their credit cards for almost two years, yet their debt continues to increase from monthly late payment fees and a percentage rate of almost 24% APR. . . . I believe that it is unconscionable for these bankcards to take advantage of a college student's youth and inexperience. They are ignoring their own sound banking practices by changing the rules just to benefit themselves. You just cannot have it both ways. Banks cannot state in their contract that falsely representing one's creditworthiness is a crime and then turn around and give credit to one who is not creditworthy when it suits their own financial benefit. As professionals with the public trust, they have the responsibility not to ignore their own rules.

Ruth Susswein, of Bankcard Holders of America, testified that "The student who racks up a $1000 credit card bill her freshman year, and only pays the low, low minimum payment each month, will finish her Bachelor's degree, complete her Masters program, finally begin earning a living, and *still* have three and a half years to go to finish paying off that freshman spending spree—and that assumes this student stopped charging after she spent

$1000 nearly nine years earlier." Visa and MasterCard were there too, back to talk about adulthood. The Visa representative contended, "The unyielding commitment and resolve of Visa and its members to consumer education is a prime example, not of marketing but of social responsibility. Our goal—and our responsibility—is to treat college students as fully franchised adults, first and foremost by giving them the tools they need to function as such."[18] And Gary Flood, senior vice president of MasterCard, borrowed from anthropology to echo his colleague's assertion: "Many of these students take the opportunity to apply for credit cards and view obtaining a credit card as an important part of the financial rite of passage into adulthood."[19]

Gary Flood used the anthropological concept of a rite of passage, the social drama produced when members of a community come together to celebrate a person's transition to a new social role. The rite of passage proceeds through three stages. First, separation: one leaves behind an old social role. Then you enter a liminal stage, where you are neither your old self nor a new one, but between selves, somewhat like standing on the threshold of a door. In the third and final stage, you are reborn, but as a different person, with a new set of rights and responsibilities.[20] The rite of passage resembles a hero's quest. Joseph Campbell wrote that these same three steps help define and provide understanding for the journeys of heroes, from Ulysses through Superman.[21] Rites of passage do more than express change; they make change happen. In this section, I will illustrate Gary Flood's metaphor with quotations from students interviewed by Angela Guerra and Gina Pearson in 1995. Although their paths diverge, they all trace the contours of a spoiled rite of passage, or a hero's thwarted quest: from an illusory leap into adulthood and autonomy, through a period of gathering debt, past a crisis of some sort and a debtors' graduation paralleling their college commencement, then settling into an adult life saddled with seemingly intractable debt. Students' insights show how cleverly credit card issuers tapped into the difficulties of making the transition to adulthood in the 1990s, and how much they damaged students' lives. Although most students bring to this spoiled journey a familiarity with credit cards, their experiences vary enormously. For some, their parents' debts left a mark; for others using credit cards seemed natural.

I. SEPARATION: THE CREDIT CARD

Students received their first credit cards in two ways: as a gift from their families for emergencies while away from home, or through university-based solicitors.

Megan, a nineteen-year-old woman from Connecticut:

October of my freshman year was when I first got my credit card, and it was a Citibank MasterCard. I found the pamphlets that they were offering it to students, and I have my loans from them, so I decided to keep it all in the same bank.

I was very excited, I couldn't wait!!! That was like a few days before I went on my shopping spree! I was all excited, and it was great. I felt more adult too. I was away from the house, I had my own credit cards, and I was like, WhooHoo!!! A wave of independence swept over me. I felt like a real adult with a real credit card, able to make real choices.

Sarah, a nineteen-year-old woman from Maryland:

I thought it was cool, you know, my very own Visa card, and I went around show-ing everyone, but it was exciting, but I wasn't in awe of it or anything, it was just ex-citing to have if I needed it. With cash, you never know if you have enough . . . with credit you always have enough, to charge and think and live better now.

I think that being away from home has a lot to do with it, and I don't think that the companies need to be as aggressive as they are. Because, you know, they're a lit-tle enticing, and I think that's out of line. I think that there are very few people who really, really, need a credit card. I think that probably I don't need my credit card, but it's nice to have . . . convenient, it makes things easier, but I don't really need it. I don't have to have a credit card.

While separation was a thrill for some, for others it was not necessarily an operative factor.

Alan, a twenty-year-old business major from New Jersey:

I pay attention to credit card ads every once in a while. But it seems like they're all fighting each other, and they're all established in history already. Amex is fighting Visa, and MasterCard is fighting them all. Ads aren't going to change that. . . . Amex and company are still the elite cards, and Visa comes second to that for me. And MasterCard comes third. The [ad] that I remember is the Amex one with Jerry Seinfeld in it . . . makes sense to me because it was trying to tell you to take power and control of the situation. What I didn't like about it was: A credit card is con-trolling you? Or are you controlling the credit card?

I first got a credit card in October. It was not a big deal to me. I had the feeling that I would get it, because it's not like I had a tarnished credit history, or even a touched credit history. If I got it, I got it. If I didn't, I didn't. I would then have my parents' credit card to fall back on. It was more like a snobbish response because of the indifference, but it was like they needed me more than I needed them.

II. Liminality

Megan:

I mainly used them for the holidays, and I paid my phone bills with it. I buy toiletries with it, I've bought groceries with it, I order from catalogues with it a lot, and I've used it for books too. Mostly clothes and toiletries, I haven't really bought any appliances, I've used it more for other people's presents than for myself.

Sarah:

I got my entire family sweatshirts from the campus store, and they're about $50 each, and there's no way that I would have laid down $200 cash. . . . I'm much more likely to buy with the credit card, because without it, I just wouldn't have the cash, and I wouldn't be able to buy it at all. When there is room on the card for spending, the individual could not possibly be broke.

Alan:

Credit cards influence my shopping because holding this piece of plastic, this annoying piece of plastic, it's like a magnet. Yes, I want this. . . . And I'll buy because I have the credit available on the card, and I'll avoid paying for it until the bill comes due. If I didn't have a credit card, I wouldn't be doing the kind of shopping that I normally do. I'm more likely to buy because of them. I hesitate a lot more now, because of some of the investing that I'm doing, but I used to not. In fact, now I'm not even carrying any credit cards with me. . . . I keep them secure, unless I know that I'm going to need them.

III. Rebirth

Crisis can end the fun, or it can propel students deeper into debt. Sometimes universities reduce or discontinue financial aid by a student's junior year so that they can offer aid packages to incoming students.[22] Predictable life changes can precipitate a turning point: reaching twenty-one, graduating from college, having to support yourself. Sometimes parents cut off their children earlier, because they are in their own difficult financial straits. Health problems, layoffs, and sending more children to college can all set families back. Sometimes students move and miss a bill, while at other times the crisis is debt-driven: you exceed your credit limit, or the bank raises your limit without your knowledge, and you continue to charge or simply cannot manage the increased payments. You lose your job or have an accident or unexpected bills. You can find your expenses up and income down. A friend borrows your card and is unable to pay you back later.

Alan:

Well, when I first got my credit card, I always paid in full. However, working Christmas break, I didn't make as much money as I anticipated, so I'm paying off those debts Because like I said, I didn't make the money expected.

Plus, I did some extra clothes shopping, plus I took some friends out for an extraordinary weekend, which was completely unnecessary, but fun all the same. Ever since February, I've been paying off in increments; recently I paid one credit card off in full and I'm about half-way through the other one, and the third credit card, I've hardly touched, because it has the lowest interest rate. After I solve this problem of paying off the credit card I will never do this again, because I've never had this problem, and never want to have it again. I've never missed a payment, although I'm going to let one lapse for a few days, but that's because I'm leaving to go home, I'll pay it once I go home, and I've been given permission by the company to do so.

Megan:

Somewhere during this transition, my credit cards became a necessity for me. I was charging a sandwich a day to eat, keeping my money in my bank account for rent only. I had absolutely no cash, even though I was working 30 hours a week. Half of my earnings goes to pay the minimum of each of my credit card bills. Most of my accounts have been handed over to collection agencies. I wrote letters explaining the situation to every company. I gave them copies of the accident report and my medical bills as proof. I dread answering the phone, so I have my girlfriend screen my calls. I've come to hate getting the mail. All I seem to get are threats from the collection agency.

If I think about it, I'll just get depressed. All I worry about is maintaining my juggling act with the collection agencies until everything is settled. Of course the next thing I'll have to worry about is reestablishing my credit rating.

I realized 45 percent of my income was going to service my debt. It's like a ghost that comes back to haunt you. There's always a mental cost, because there's some nights when I have panic attacks, because I think that I have this $550 debt, and I wonder about how I'm going to pay it back. So I guess that it's more of a cost on my brain, and I have less cash because some of that paycheck has to go to paying my credit card bill. I always have to allot a certain amount of each pay period to go to that.

A chasm grew between what students knew and what they experienced, mirroring the out-of-synch role of credit and debt in American life, the

crack between what we have and what we own and do. Building credit became almost as important as building a portfolio or a transcript.

Megan:

I want to learn more self control with them, because I know that I'll have the credit
sometimes, and that I can just pay it off later. But, I'm sure that I'll use them in the
future, because you know, you never have enough cash for everything and I'm hoping that it'll be giving me a good credit history, so that when I want to buy a house
or a car or something, that they'll look at my credit as being good.

Alan:

They've given me a credit history. By having this debt problem, it's taught me something about debt management, and budgeting and expense management. I'm now
using the budget system, whereby, before, I knew how much I had allocated for a
certain month, but now I reallocate the funds. So it has helped me in that way. I expect to get out of my credit card debt within the next year, if not the next five
months, that's a problem. I have other debts, though.

Students' shadow careers of debt haunted their journeys through college.
The system that entrapped them originally did not scare or concern them.
The concept of "usury" did not resonate. The headiness that came with the
power to spend combined with their sense that debt was inevitable and their
very real cash poverty drowned out the admonitions about prudence and
savings that were staples of previous generations. Students groped for other
metaphors and a strange new language to talk about what was happening
to them: debt appeared like a mountain of dirt, or sludge, built by
"chunks," as they "charged up to the sky," it "grows and grows," and they
tried to "pay it down" or "spread it out."

Megan:

I think that they've definitely affected my shopping. Just today, I knew that I had just
paid the bill, and so I could go buy something else because I had just paid that bill
to them. Because I have more credit now. It makes me buy things that I think I
would never buy. It's so easy just to swipe it through that I rarely hesitate. There's
some things that I wish that I hadn't charged, because I think that my train ticket,
now is a $150 chunk in my credit. But there's other things that I think I had to, be-
cause I didn't have the cash.

These students neither embraced nor repudiated dominant cultural meanings about credit and debt. Rather, they juggled confused feelings of entitlement, gratitude, remorse, and rage against their varied lived experiences of middle-class status and, for some, downward mobility.

Sarah said:

There have been several times I felt grateful, like when I was sick. You know, my medicine was like $60 for two prescriptions, and when I went to get them, I didn't have like an extra $60 sitting around my checking account and so I was thankful that I had my credit card, because without it, I wouldn't have been able to get my medicine. And, actually, I think that I only ended up spending $30, because I was afraid that my credit card wasn't going to clear, because I thought that I was above my limit. Well, it did clear, because that way I got my medicine. And when my friend was here if I wouldn't have been able, I mean, she had money, but not enough to pay for both of us, and there was no other place to eat, and we wouldn't have been able to eat for eight days, because I had *no cash*. So there were a lot of times when I was thankful that I had it. . . . I personally don't like credit card debt and that's why I'm making a point to pay it off by the end of the summer, and that's why I'm kind of apprehensive about paying it back as soon as possible, even before I save money for books. Because I can always buy them with the money that I make here, once I get back. But I'm definitely going to pay it off, because I don't want it to get out of hand.

I know that credit card companies make a lot, a lot of money and it seems to me that the interest is pretty steep. I can't remember offhand if my credit card interest is 14.98 percent or 15.98 percent, I'm pretty sure that it's 15.98 percent, and I think that's pretty steep. I mean, it's not bad if you only have $100 on your credit card, but obviously the more you have, the more you pay. And like I said, I have $500 on my credit card now, and they structure my minimum, I mean, I probably wouldn't be able to pay much more on my minimum more than I do now, but they structure my minimum so that I only pay one-third of the interest every time that I make a credit card payment and so then I pay, but it goes down a little, and then it's compounded again, so that . . . I remember getting one credit card bill, and then paying it, and my next bill was even higher than the first. So I owed more money than before, even after I made the payment. It's kind of like a never ending battle in a sense, because no matter how much you pay, you can never get out because you always owe more the next time you have to pay. I think that they issue credit cards because it's a lucrative business for one thing, I think that they can make a lot of money in the trade and that's probably the main reason. That's the reason that they're in the banking business: to make money. So I would assume, I mean I don't think that they do it with a vicious intent, entrenching all these people in this horrible debt that they can't get out.

Megan:

The interest that I pay doesn't seem fair, because it seems like so much because I know that if I only send the minimum that it builds up, but now that they've lowered it, it makes me feel like since I've paid it timely, they'll reward me. They've made me really have a nice Christmas for my family and boyfriend, and they've made me feel that if I ever really need something that I'll have a way to pay for it, and that's kind of nice.

Sarah:

I think that they are just out to make money, like any other business, but I think that there's a lot of problems with . . . people getting into huge debts. But in a sense I don't think that that really is the credit card company's responsibility, because they're out making money and that's their business, and it's up to the people who have credit cards to use them intelligently and to be able to manage their own behavior. . . . I don't really fault credit card companies, I mean, they may portray an image of, you know, you can buy whatever you want and then pay for it later, but it's kind of like being an informed consumer, you don't always believe what the advertisements tell you and you have to do it on your own.

Like everyone else, these students could talk about their "credit others," those people they imagined abusing credit.

Sarah:

I think that my parents abuse cards to a certain extent. And I think that there's a significant portion of people who have credit cards who abuse them. I mean, you hear stories or see TV shows about people who are compulsive shoppers, and that's kind of like, credit cards do nothing but help those people. If they didn't have it, I mean because those people did the same thing writing bad checks, they'd be thrown in jail for that. But it makes it much easier for people to do that with credit cards, and I think there's a lot of abuse out there.

I think the lower-middle class, or working class maybe types of people abuse credit cards. Who want to be upwardly mobile but don't have the money to do it. I think they use credit cards for that. And just buy, and pay for it later, and I think that a lot of them get in over their heads that way.

Alan:

Everyone abuses credit cards. They spend beyond their limits . . . at least most people. Everyone does it. There's certain people who know better. For example, my mother just charges and charges and charges, but my father, he knows better and will only charge something if he needs it, and he does that once or twice a year. The person who's paying the bills is usually more unlikely to spend, because they're saving for the future. Unfortunately, it's their spouses.

Also, like other debtors, members of this generation vary by the class inequalities that help shape their experiences and perceptions.

Alan:

I've been using credit card since I was 11, I've been handling my parents' credit cards when I go shopping for myself. I've seen my parents use credit cards all my life, though. They used them for just about everything, they used them for clothes, accessories for the house, pool accessories, basically everything it can be used for except groceries and food, because they refuse to use them for that. Today, I have four credit cards. In terms of prestige, I have my parents' gold card, which is in my parents' name. All of my cards have different limits, and different terms. They've raised my limit without my asking.

I use my credit cards for different things. I use them to take my friends out to dinner, or to the theater, and stuff like that. I use them to go clothes shopping, and for other things. I do use them for grocery shopping. Basically I use them for necessities of life. I purchased upgrades to my computer. I purchased various un-necessities, like CDs or clothes, or picture frames, books, electronics.

Sarah:

It was like once my dad didn't have money, he started spending more, and he put it all on the credit card because it wasn't "real money." And now they're going to be paying that back forever, unless they win the lottery or something. I mean, $35,000 takes a long time to pay off, I would probably give them 20–25 years before they get it paid off, if they ever do. And they're still using them, but not as much. There's certain cards that they never use, like the Visa, but there are other cards, like the Dillard's card, that's the worst. They probably owe $2,700 on that alone and they charge things on it because my mother likes to shop. I don't think that she's still shopping, and my father doesn't use them unless it's something big. They also have to pay for college now, and so that's affected them too. . . . I mean my parents got into a lot of trouble with their credit cards, I guess they owe about $35,000 on their credit cards, and that includes gas cards, store cards, and the like. And that hurts me a lot, because of financial aid reasons, I mean, there's no space on the form for credit card debt. They see that my parents make $65,000 a year, but there's no place for outstanding debts. But a lot of that happened because my father was out of work

.bout a year, and we basically lived off the credit cards. So I kind of have an an-
.nosity towards it.

These students' stories help illuminate the problem of aggressively marketing credit cards on college campuses. The students try to untangle the
system of credit and debt, but it is sometimes hard for them to do so. They
are not mindless pawns or giddy consumers, but they are vulnerable: to fine
print, temptation, scapegoating, emergencies, and a sudden change of fortune . . .

Student Loans

Education has long been the centerpiece of the American Dream, crucial
to democracy for building an informed and thoughtful citizenry, central to
Jefferson's belief in equality of opportunity, prized as a path out of poverty.
Education has long been a site of struggle for people who were denied
equal access to schools, teachers, and learning resources. The GI Bill of
Rights, Brown vs. the Board of Education, and the Higher Education Act
of 1965 all affirmed public responsibility for increasingly accessible education for all.

Kenesaw Landis wrote of the segregated schools of Washington, D.C.:

The public school system has been the great instrument by which we hoped to over-
come inequalities of birth and station, and give each American an equal chance to
make good. It has been the great unifying principle of the Republic. When the public schools of the capital are used instead to divide citizens or racial lines, to perpet-
uate inequalities, to increase them, and worse to justify them, then the time has
come to consider what kind of an American we want to build for the future.[23]

The civil rights movement, the Great Society, and the War on Poverty of
the 1960s have haunted the student loan movement, which has turned the
grant to loan ratios of the 1960s upside down. Needy students in the 1960s
were far more likely to receive grants for college than loans. Today they are
much more likely to receive loans than grants. Although the details of student loan politics and administration may appear tedious and picayune,
they illuminate larger, changing, contested ideals about education, equality,
and access.

In 1965, the Higher Education Act provided loans for lower- to middle-
income students with lower interest than ordinary bank loans. The government made these loans itself, because banks were not interested in
committing loans to education. In the student loan drama, banks seem like
bullies: they won't play, they threaten to walk away, they do walk away, then

they're angry when they lose, for student loans are their most profitable portfolio next to credit cards and some industrial loans. Student loans are more profitable, for example, than a car loan or a mortgage. But this wasn't obvious in 1965.[24]

In 1972, under President Nixon, the government created the National Student Loan Marketing Association. We know this association more familiarly as Sallie Mae. For some reason we name her as though she were a little southern girl rather than a greedy middleman run by exorbitantly-paid men. But in the Sallie Mae story, names are never what they mean. The Coalition for Student Loan Reform is a trade group of guaranty agencies, not a student group,[25] and the HEAA is a guaranty agency that breathes down your neck to police your loan. John Heilemann calls her Sallie Mayhem and the executives Sallie Maestros.[26] Sallie Mae was supposed to be liberating, enabling, to make higher education more accessible. I believe it may be a racket. I refer to her as Sal, so she can sound like a character on "The Sopranos."

This is how it is supposed to work. Sal raises money on the financial markets, where it can borrow money at very low interest. This is because it is a government sponsored enterprise and therefore the government guarantees its loans through our taxes. Then Sal advances money to private banks like Citicorp and Chase Chemical. The students borrow the money, usually through their colleges, to pay the tuition. The government pays the bank the interest on the loan while the student is in school. Then, when the student graduates, the bank can sell the loan back to Sal, which sells the loan back on the financial markets, or it can keep the loan and do the collecting itself. The student has to start paying the loan back with interest six months after leaving school. If the student cannot make the payments, the government pays the bank, or whoever owns the loan, back. Every transaction has a little profit. This seems like complicated trafficking in student debt; in any case it is enormously profitable to Sallie Mae and to banks, and it is risk free, because the taxpayers guarantee to the bank that it will not have to waste time trying to collect bad loans, that it will always be paid back.

Sal is weird. It has stockholders who make profits. It invests in interest producing debt, rather than something more productive that might build something. It pays no taxes. It is one of the top 100 corporations in the country, and its executives earn huge salaries. Student loans have provided corporate welfare for banks and have been especially lucrative for the biggest banks, Citicorp and Chase, for whom they are its third most profitable lending venture, out producing mortgages and car loans. I'm not sure why student loans, President Johnson's brainstorm to open up higher education just like the GI Bill, should be so profitable.[27]

During the 1980s, as families grew more indebted and desperate, the loan program endured several skirmishes and changed a little over time. In 1986, students won the right to consolidate their loans and fix the interest they paid, which would be capped at 8.25 percent for the whole ten years of payback. Critics worried that this could become a gravy train for higher-income students, who would ride out their loans at low interest when they could afford to pay more.[28] In 1989 Sal decided not to guarantee loans that banks made to trade schools where the default rate was more than 60 percent. "[It is] inherently less profitable," said Stephen Iovino, president of Chase Manhattan's student-loan unit. That's because it costs as much to process and carry a $2,500 loan to a proprietary-school student as it does to make a $10,000 loan to an Ivy League student.[29]

High tuition and family debt powered Sal's growth.[30] All together the Reagan years witnessed more eligible students, needier families, steep and unpredictable tuition increases, more borrowing, and the growth of profits from student loans.[31] Terry Hartle and Fred Galloway of the American Council on Education point out that "average tuition and fees at all Massachusetts public institutions have risen by over 110 percent in the last five years; nationwide, tuition at four-year public institutions has increased by nearly 48% In fiscally strapped California, tuition and fees at public four-year colleges jumped by 75% from 1990–91 to 1992–93."

Reflecting on the unique qualities of student loans, anthropologist Bev Salehi wrote,

With most long-term debts, the borrower is able to calculate total costs and interest rates, and the decision to borrow is based on some knowledge of the borrower's projected income and expenses. However, when students borrow to finance their education, they take on debt incrementally and they cannot know at any point either the full price of the education or what the real burden of the debt they are assuming will be. With the current high levels of annual tuition increases, students' expenses can rise dramatically while they are still in school. Moreover, students have no way of knowing what their future job prospects will be or even whether they will graduate.[32]

This indeterminate character of the loan is even more true today, as students receive unwieldy financial aid packages, with a hodgepodge of loans and grants from many sources and a changing panoply of bureaucrats who administer, process, monitor, and collect payments on the loans.[33]

In 1992 Sal came up for reauthorization by Congress. When the reauthorization was passed, a single application was developed for all financial aid, the maximum a student could borrow was raised to $23,000, and anybody could apply for an unsubsidized loan, regardless of one's ability to pay the loan back.

When President Clinton came to office in 1993, he considered reforming student loans his showpiece program. He wanted to institute direct lending by the government to bypass the banks, income contingent repayment over a longer period of time, and national service or useful but ill-paid work to pay back part of the loan.[34] Clinton believed in assuring access to higher education without terrible indebtedness. Senators Ted Kennedy and Paul Simon sponsored the proposed changes. They argued that Sallie Mae was greedy and unnecessary and that lenders exploited needy students for profit. To simplify the system, they wanted the Department of Education to lend the money directly and the IRS to collect on an income-contingency basis. Therefore a social worker or a minister would not have to make the same monthly payment as a more highly paid lawyer or a doctor. If debtors went into national service or a public service job they could get some of their debt forgiven.

Sal's stock plummeted. Corporate lobbyists swore to stamp out reform. They expressed outrage that Clinton, who was supposed to be a centrist and who had promised them public-private partnerships, would dare suggest that government might be more efficient than corporations. They chastised the president for wanting to replace "well-run private businesses with an even more bloated government bureaucracy!"[35] One asked, "Will it turn around and use that loan authority to dictate tuition controls, cap registration fees or mandate a Politically Correct national curriculum?"[36] They were upset that the Department of Education was going to hire 600 employees "when Washington has to learn to live within its means."[37] (God forbid that people should find work in the public sector.) Other opponents of reform argued alternatively that the improved terms, streamlined procedures, less burdensome paperwork, and documentation constituted unfair competition.

In the compromise Congress worked out, government was to become the direct lender of 5 percent of all loans and build slowly to half or more. Universities could choose between the government and private lenders. Some, such as Pennsylvania State, reported pressure not to subscribe to direct government lending. In another example, USA Group of Indiana, the country's largest guaranty agency, reminded trustees at Indiana University that the health of the regional economy was linked to its own fate, and they raised the specter of mass unemployment. USA Group's president and CEO Troy Nicholson told trustees that "our national headquarters is on I-69 just north of Indianapolis. We employ more than 2,400 Hoosiers."[38]

USA Group is one of three dozen guaranty agencies that process student loans and then police them for fees paid by both government and private lenders. It also monitors banks to make sure they're diligent and creates subsidiaries, some profit and some non profit, to handle every aspect of making, administering, and collecting loans. And it just keeps growing, along with others in the field, such as EduCap. In 1996 USA Group's computer followed 37 million loans, its CEO earned a $1 million salary, four other executives earned at least $300,000, and thirty others earned $100,000.[39] In 1996 this non profit agency declared an "excess" (a profit) of more than $67 million. Complaining about this excess to the Internal Revenue Service, Senator Simon argued that "it violates the spirit, if not the letter, of the law."

Before the reforms, all student loans were on a standard ten-year repayment plan. The compromise gave students more options. If they wished, they could hook repayment to their income, so the amount due would go up and down with their salary at different times. They could take as long as thirty years to repay the loan.[40] They could consolidate their multiple loans into one loan and fix it at a low interest rate. These reforms sparked more debate: student groups argued that the thirty-year payment program only made college *seem* more affordable. With interest, you were actually paying as much as double or triple the actual cost. It would spin out of control and be like a second mortgage, without the house, argued James Appleberry, president of the American Association of State Colleges and Universities. United States Student Association lobbyist Laura McClintock added that it smacked of a credit card scheme, offering the lure of low monthly payments in exchange for mounting debt. Lower payments really meant larger debt.[41]

On November 3, 1994, the *Washington Post* wrote that the *Clinton* plan "merely reflects the reality of a shift in the magnitude of the college tuition burden—as the President put it, from something like a consumer good, which you save up for[,] pay for[,] and then use—to something like a mortgage, in which you invest and then pay off over time." Bev Salehi noted, "This curious distinction between a consumer good and an investment paid for over time ignores the fact that in our credit-driven economy most of us go on paying for consumer goods long after they have become useless or obsolete. With millions of workers anxiously investing in higher levels of education to remain marketable in an unstable labor market, education is quickly becoming the ultimate consumer good."[42] (Some time around then, college operators began calling themselves customer service representatives, and colleges began referring to students as customers.) But the immediate, tangible effect was a surge in student loan borrowing, which, in the next two years totaled more than all student loans in the 1960s, 1970s, and 1980s combined.[43]

Each time the student loan reauthorization comes before Congress, different members try to attach amendments for various kinds of reform. The conservative Contract with America went after the Clinton plan hard, hoping to remove remedial coursework from loans guaranteed by government, waving the banner of the undeserving poor who were unlikely to repay the money.[44] In 1998 Congress voted to deny federal aid to students convicted of marijuana possession, but not murder or rape. Withholding financial aid has been used to discipline teen mothers and political protesters.[45] Legal immigrants have been penalized. For example, in 1996, Congress voted to count an immigrant's sponsor's income as part of the income of the immigrant student applicant. Many of these amendments hurt poor and minority students as well as anyone attending a trade school or community college.[46]

Reauthorization comes up again in 2004, and a rainbow of politicized amendments are already attached—to forbid aid to hazers, to take away the in-school interest subsidy, to forgive $5000 of your debt if you teach in Head Start or work in other fields that serve low-income clients or the government.[47] President Bush hopes to shave $1.3 billion off the federal deficit at the expense of students by making it illegal to consolidate a loan at a low interest rate. Also, the administration wants to slash AmeriCorps, the vestige of Clinton's national service program, although volunteers in this program receive only $4725 toward higher education. Some members of Congress hope to eliminate work-study programs, which could shatter opportunities for many Americans to attend college. The administration hopes to lay the blame for expensive education on universities and impose stringent cost-cutting measures where possible. Accreditation measures would include graduation rates, another index and engine of inequality for students who have to work to pay for their education.[48]

Rather than providing equality of opportunity, education reflects and reproduces the inequality of our time, and students' credit card debt both complements and pales next to the student loan debt they carry into adulthood. Student loan debt exacerbates the effects of SAT scores, and even early admissions, when wealthier students for whom financial aid isn't a deal breaker can negotiate to attend the elite colleges of their choice. College tuition has been increasing for twenty-five years. It has quadrupled since 1977. Financial aid, especially loans, has been increasing too. More family income is committed to college: for the poor the portion has risen from 13 percent in 1980 to 25 percent in 2000. In 2002 the gap between tuition costs and grants kept 48 percent of students from families earning less than $25,000 out of four-year colleges and 43 percent of those whose families earned between $25,000 and $50,000. Student borrowers take on an avrage of $27,600 in educational debt to graduate.[49]

In 2000, every state raised tuition and fees for public universities, and twenty-six states cut their higher education budgets. It appeared that public universities could only survive by becoming more private. People in different financial circumstances have responded in varied ways to these changes. Some don't want to borrow at all. Others go to trade school, or community college, or drop out to work full-time when unemployment hits their families. Or they drop out temporarily and tread water after their student loan debt kicks in after six months. Or they stay in school but major in business rather than the liberal arts or social work.[50]

John Heilemann writes, "Forget working as a doctor at a free clinic in Anacostia; or heading to Central America for Catholic Relief Services; or working as a house painter while you write a book of poetry; or starting a program like Teach for America. With any of these jobs, you'll be in default before you can say "slacker."[51]

When Jason Fetter interviewed the young man vending credit cards on our quad on September 11, 1995, this was his report:

I interviewed Charlie on the quad. He presently resides in King George, Virginia. After graduating from Johns Hopkins with a major in Biology, he completed one year of medical school. He's been working for credit card companies for almost two years. . . . Although he was vending credit cards to students the day I interviewed him, he usually gives seminars on credit cards. The typical day consists of eight hours, usually on one campus. Throughout the year, the salespeople rotate to various campuses across the country. The pay is according to the number of applications in a given day, and there are no quotas they are required to fill. When first hired, Charlie like many others began with phone training in soliciting credit cards, followed by on site training. Charlie said that most people work seven days a week and in a good week he will make around eight hundred dollars. In a one-day period, they vended about one hundred applications in a four-hour time period at the American University. . . . Charlie vends for Mobile Gas, Sunoco, AT&T, and Discover Cards.

Gabriel's story helps illuminate the way student loans can affect the life of a bright, insightful college student:

At first it was kind of like how much I make, my entire salary for the next few years, I'd have to get a 50,000 dollar job, more realistic, I'll get 35,000, and all that will do is cover my debt, assuming that I have no other bills to pay, all I can do is cover my debt. So the fact that I'm already in the red getting out of college kind of makes me wonder if I should have taken a year or two off, maybe gone to a cheaper school, because basically I paid for the reputation. Plus it was drilled through our heads, I mean all through high school, the better school you go to the better chance you have of getting a good job . . . and I'm thinking I could have gone to Maryland, stayed in state, or any other school for a lot cheaper and I know I could have gotten just as good an education. . . . I got friends going to Montgomery College getting just as good an education—it's not like N is that much better. College is pretty much what you put into it. You kind of force yourself to go to classes, whatever, but if I could have gone all over again I probably would have taken a year or two off, gone to a lot cheaper school, graduated with a lot less debt. My graduate degree is much more important.

I was just like, whatever, the top school you can get into, go for it. No matter what. If I'd gone to Harvard, Yale, whatever, I would have graduated with $100,000 worth of debt from there, that would have been better than graduating with $5,000 worth of debt from Indiana University. It was, alright, my freshman year I came in, I had grants, loans, private loans, government loans, and then my junior year [his mother died] me and my pops kinda fell out, or whatever, so I was pretty much on my own. So I was getting a little help from my dad, so I went back to school and explained my situation, and they boosted my aid, not really so much in grants, but they gave me a lot more private loans, I got another private loan from Sallie Mae, basically I increased my loans. I didn't know the kind of debt I was getting myself into.

Basically, just getting by. My sophomore year wasn't as bad as my senior year. My senior year, my credit was already messed up, but somehow I got a platinum card. So I killed that, in no time. When you're a college student, I mean you're so broke, especially when you get through with paying for books, and all that other stuff, and you know when you're going out and you got a card right there? Makes things a lot easier, whether I'm going to see a movie, or concerts, whatever, you know what I mean? I remember I charged 4 or 500 dollars on books one time, and that was just one semester.

I mean I talked once with an admission counselor and she pretty much just gave me the basics, but I was pretty much just reading for myself, the paperwork. Especially that last year, my senior year, once I was on my own, everything on my shoulders. And everything kind of was before, but at least my dad was helping me out, covering some of the tuition. But once I was really on my own I had to actually sit there and kind of think what I was getting myself into. But even then I can't say I know exactly how much I owe, how much monthly it's supposed to be. Sallie Mae is 50 a month, federal and Perkins is probably somewhere around 50 a month . . .

They been harassing me since forever. I mean, like my cell phone, I'm like how did y'all find the numbers where I'm at, I mean they were harassing me at work, I mean it was ridiculous, I'm like how did y'all get this number? They're a lot worse . . . They called me at work, and that's embarrassing. They be all slick, hey won't even be like Mr. W—or something like that, it's hey let me talk to Gabe, or G, talk about they're taking you to court, every single day they call you. Talking about they want to take me to court, I mean like every single day. . . . They been calling the house, my pops say they've been calling the house constantly, my credit's so messed up at this point, I have no job right now, so that's the last thing on my mind is worrying about that. I'm more concerned about immediate bills like rent, stuff like that . . . a long time. Like forever I think it's ten, fifteen years, a long time, a long time, I probably won't be through with my debt till I'm in my mid to late 30s.

He talked about the work he'd done since graduating:

I was doing clerical bullshit. There's a market room where the traders were making their trades. I was working in there. I was cool, sitting behind a desk, always hectic and fast-paced. But I'm basically their little helper. Their little gofer. Answer the phones, file, copy, fax machines, that kind of stuff. I mean I was a contractor. If you're a contractor, they can replace you just like that. Honestly, I couldn't afford to have [health insurance] taken out of my check. Because I was literally living on my own, I was staying with my cousin in Silver Spring for awhile. Once I had my own place every dollar counts. I've gotta pay bills here, bills there, and I hadn't even started paying my college debt. I knew, come June, I was gonna need to start making those payments. So I thought I could get by a year without insurance. I could risk a year or two.

I was selling coupons. You know, like Papa Johns, say a $25 card gets you 2 free pizzas, once you buy one you get one free. Or restaurants a basic coupon covers, you purchase the card for 20, 30 bucks something like that, you come in, you eat lunch for free, you're like half off, basically coupons for a whole bunch of food places. They're so good, man, they're so good. (Plus I never would have know this if I hadn't took the rhetoric class at N.) Basically every morning you get a motivational speech. And they keep on selling us the dream. I know it's hard now, but if you keep on six months you'll own your own business eventually they'll come up with this little . . . like for example the law of averages 1 out of 10 people will purchase your product. For every nine people that say no to you can put a dollar in my pocket. Cause you get ten dollars for every sale you make. For every 9 nos the tenth one's gonna be a yes. That's a dollar in my pocket. They're positive ways to get through the day. They'll be like think about the bigger picture, don't worry about the insignificant nos, cause out of every hundred people you see 90 of them are going to say no, and you have to let that slide. And we'd have meetings every day, every morning, and they'd be like without hard work, without sacrifice, there's no struggle, there's no success, they'll be reading quotes from like Thoreau and all these famous authors, I mean like every morning. Cause they know they gotta keep selling that dream for us to get over the fact we get a door slammed in our face every day.

When I first got in, I was motivated, I was excited, I was doing okay, making like $300 a week. But I see the only reason I really took the job is because it was the only one available and number two because it's straight commission you don't get any salary whatsoever, since it's straight commission you keep whatever you make that day. So I was thinking, I need to cheat the system, because I'm broke right now, and the way I got laid off, I need to take advantage of everything I could get.

If I file for unemployment and they see me getting a check, I think somehow they can trace that, or eventually it will catch up to me. But if I'm getting straight cash, or straight commission, I can still say I'm unemployed and still get that money. So hopefully with the unemployment and me making whatever little money I make from door to door sales, it will add up.

He would like to have a better job:

I mean I haven't given up, but the thing is I really want to work for an ad agency. I even know what position I want to be. I want to be the copywriter, the one who comes up with the commercials. That's interesting to me. I always wanted to get into media; I want to be in the entertainment business, whether it be music, sports, the business side of it, whether it be marketing, promotion. Right now, I really want to work for an ad agency, but the thing is, remember when I said I never interned for an agency before. And in a tough job market that's the first thing they look for. They could care less if I went to Harvard. If I don't have any agency experience, they won't hire me. It's so tough getting my foot in the door. I can't even get a secretarial position. . . . I'm not giving up. I've been through way too much to give up, you know what I'm saying? Especially just getting through college, especially once me and my pops stopped getting along and I was sitting there kind of on my own. Basically N wanted me to take a year off and I knew if I took that year off I wouldn't finish, so I had to get it just for me going through that whole year I mean I was broke. That's part of the reason why I got in that little trouble towards the end of the year, once my loans dried out, once the money was all dried up, I was eating one meal a day, trying to get by on 50 dollars a week. I was living with the football team, like a big house. I was only paying $300 a month, staying in a room and I was living at the bare minimum, okay I'll go ahead and say it on tape, I was stealing my books because I knew someone who worked in a bookstore, so I had her hook me up with a whole bunch of books.

He has strong feelings about politics, although he does not quite connect them to his frustration with his debt:

I don't know whose fault it is, but I know who's not making it better, is President Bush. I don't see how that idiot got up in office in the first place, he needed to cheat at the election or whatever. But still, the fact that he's about to get reelected is ridiculous. I mean, can't stand him. I know this has been said a hundred times, but he's so worried about abroad when all you got to do is look out the back of the White House. I mean look in Northeast, look in Southeast, look at all of DC a matter of fact, and there's guys out here starving, you know what I'm saying, take care of home before you worry about other peoples' issues. And I'm not saying we should ignore third world countries, I mean I'm African, I mean I'm from Kenya, so countries who really need aid, yeah I support that. But when it comes to bombing Iraq, and everyone knows it's a war for oil, when it comes to stuff like that, that's what I get mad at. When they spend more money on defense when we already have the biggest army, times ten, when we can pretty much crush anyone, cut back some of that money you're spending on defense and give it to some of the schools. I read in a book they spend more money on locking people up than they do educating people. The DC public schools is fucked up, I mean a lot of public schools is fucked up, I've seen Chicago public schools, New York public schools, DC public schools. . . . When you're spending more money on defense and worrying about other peoples' problems than at home, that's what gets me mad. And the fact that we were already spending a ridiculous amount, and then he increased it even more with all that Homeland Security bullshit.

I didn't follow the trip to Africa, because I know that all it is is photo ops. I've been to Kenya; I used to go every other year. I seen my cousins, I've been on both sides of the fence. I went to school with a bunch of rich white kids, but I've seen my own family living in mud huts, half of them without electricity, just dirt poor, then when a president comes by and waves around and acts like he's doing something when he's not doing anything.

Many people in Gabriel's position find they must go to graduate school, not only to defer their debt payments, but also to increase their chances of landing a job. By 2002 the rising unemployment rate for college graduates was reminiscent of the job loss experienced by factory workers in the early 1980s. Some of the reasons were the same, as jobs in radiology, software design, and even creating Power Point presentations shifted overseas to countries with lower wages such as India and the Philippines. The shift in financial service jobs—anything not requiring face to face contact—was particularly harsh. The financial services industry predicted a job loss of 500,000, or 8 percent of its workforce by 2008.

However, increased eduation can be an expensive, and, for some, prohibitive path. Graduate and professional students have endured a blast of borrowing since 1992, and they especially suffer from the burden of adding this extra debt on to the undergraduate debt they already owe. They also suffer from the dimished value of fellowships and assistantships (componded by the fact students are now required to pay income taxes on these monies), as well as a graduate education structure that often leaves their last few years toward the degree unfunded. On top of this, there is a scarcity of good paying, high growth professions available to them after they receive their diploma. They mortgage their futures in the hope of doing what they love. Even those who become relatively well-paid doctors and lawyers often carry enormous debt for many years. Young people whose family backgrounds don't permit them to take on so much debt find themselves effectively closed out of these professions. Medical and law school is increasingly limited to white men whose grandparents got established in the boom years after World War II.[52]

Tony is a brilliant deejay, a saxophonist, and a life-long science whiz who majored in pre-med:

Well, I chose to go to X, just because I had family down there, it was good at science, also I was playing saxophone at the time, so I was thinking about jazz, family, and science, so New Orleans was the best way to go. . . . I got into seven schools over all. I was accepted to Rochester School of Music, I got into Hampton—Howard's rival, right? I got into Florida A and M, Xavier, that's already four. . . . I like science so much I want to reach the highest level that I can. Being a doctor, being a research, going into research or being a doctor, I kind of want to do both. I want to try every aspect of science.

I didn't really know what I was getting into . . . I thought maybe that financial aid was kind of like free money at the time. I was only doing it cause like my mom's wishes that we go through the financial aid, cause I know that me and her we talked about it over and over again but we never talked about who was going to pay it off, she was always telling me like together we'll pay it off and every time she mentioned that I would think well I don't think we ought to be paying this loan. My dad's not here. . . . I looked at it like, you know, you're not really making that much money you should just let him pay for it.

This is how I got my loans. I'm a little bitter towards the loans right now. I think my mom wanted to pay for some of my school. She wanted to pay, to put in her two cents as far as my education. So we applied for financial aid, my mom, she doesn't earn a lot, so we kind of knew we were going to get a lot of financial aid. But we didn't apply for financial aid till my third year, and we only got it for two semesters. I didn't get any grants, I got loans, one was subsidized and the other one was unsubsidized. I'm just paying back $10,000 . . . I was supposed to consolidate my interest rate . . . and I filled out some papers for it. I turned them in and then they sent them back and they told me it was incomplete for some reason. So I'm not sure what my interest rate is. . . . I let my payments pile up actually. I'm not very good with them, they're probably damaging my credit right now, but almost like $150 a month, well, no, it's two monthly payments, cause with the two different loans, one asks for $45, $50, $60, the other one asks for around the same amount, so together it's like $150 a month. That doesn't seem bad, so that's why I let it pile up. I get the check in the mail and because I write them the check every month I let the payments stand like a month or so, you know until it gets to like 300, 400 dollars, just pay the whole thing. . . . They were calling me just because they changed up their name I thought that I was dealing with three or four different agencies at one time. . . .

They might have been called EFC or CFS, or something like that. I remember that, their initials. I remember I got one letter that they said that they had had changed their company and I was like, whew, okay, I didn't know who Nelnet was.

I started getting Nelnet in the mail, and I was like, who is this. . . . I had letters stacked up and I just rubber band them, I just said I'm going to get to these later. Without just throwing them in the trash. Yeah, whenever people call my house now and they ask me if I want to consolidate my loans I just tell them I'm already working with some company, even though, . . . It's not even . . . I just feel like I'm dealing with this one group, so whoever else wants to jump in on it, I just well I've already got someone helping me out. I don't need to be confused. This Nelnet.

I looked for a job in the science field. Then I started wanting to earn a little bit of money, so I signed up for the Cutco group, like a cutlery type of thing. I went through their training program, three days, and then I wouldn't, I really didn't believe they were honest—I kind of felt like they were tricking people into buying their stuff, the whole psychology behind the dialogue, how to sell their product, I was like nobody is that serious about knives.

I'd like to go into music. All aspects though—everything—deejaying, writing music, writing lyrics, playing saxophone, studio production, all of it. . . . In school, I didn't have the money at the time to get a keyboard so I got a small mixer. It played CDs and then I started working with people who liked to rap and next thing I was like I can turn this into a money maker. And that was just contagious after that. Had the people saying you ought to go do this party, go do that party, and I got more gigs. Next thing I took over the music at X too. I was editing music, I was doing voice-overs and I was doing all the houseparties. . . . I knew coming back to DC I'm trying to not slip away, I'm just trying to regroup, it's a different scene up here, I want to come back stronger—I just haven't tried yet. Down South it's not that hard. You just play the music down there. But up here you've got to add a little . . . scratch, chop down, there it's just play the music. That was simple, everybody liked that. But up here it's harder.

So I let that go, then I had a friend tell me about this analyst position, so I tried to apply for that and she got the position, I didn't. Then I applied over at Target. I saw that they were building a Target over at Wheaton and I was waiting for it just to open. Then that just opened so quickly. So I kind of just took it and rambled. I'm working this thing called the Team. What we do, the store like gets ad sets every week, what we do, I have to give you an example, it's very hard to explain what I do. We control, we have a blueprint, of how the store is laid out, the fixtures, how the aisles are set, how all the ads work, what we do is every day, every week, we go and in and reset, it's like we do a makeover of the section in the store. And that's just how they keep a good presentation. It's not interesting, it's laid-back work, it's not challenging. At the end of the day, the job sucks, but I look at it like it's a paycheck and I have health insurance. Every time I wanted to quit, I just think, well if I quit no health insurance. My little brother's there too [He calls Target "like a sweatshop at night," because people from all over the world come to pick discarded clothing off the floor, unload the trucks, and restock the floor. He hears lots of different languages. Target is a problematic employer in several ways for him. For example, he believes that he should receive overnight pay for his 4 A.M.—noon shift, but he doesn't. He finds it hard to wake up until the lights come on at 8:00 and explains to me in detail how light affects the body.]

I ask him about politics:

silence . . . Not really, just sometimes it's hard to say because at this level I feel like I don't have control of it either way, you know, I didn't vote during the presidential election. I didn't boycott or anything, I was just lazy, but my attitude was just like it's kind of like a throw-up. Democracy is very hard to believe in that, that the people have the power. I think the next time that we probably vote, in the near future it's probably going to be like television, you know like they have reality shows? It's gonna become like that. Voting is like a joke now, especially after what happened. What I do know about politics, okay, you really have to be smart to read between the lines because the media will manipulate what you think of a candidate or what they're doing.

In today's grim economic climate, for-profit trade schools have thrived, and recruiters comb poor neighborhoods and pepper daytime TV with commercials like this one: "Do you love money—the feel of it, the smell of it, the way it sounds when you crunch it up? If green is your favorite color, we have a perfect job for you. Become a bank teller and get paid to work with money. . . . You'll be rolling in the dough before you know it."

And more students from poor homes go to vocational schools instead of colleges. Student loans were a major source of tuition revenues for trade schools, which can receive 85 percent of tuition from loans and set this tuition to correspond to the maximum amount of aid available. For-profit trade schools promise students a free education and careers as beauticians, bookkeepers, cooks, medical assistants, computer operators, truck drivers, home aides, respiratory therapists, travel agents, secretaries, and security guards. Heavily dependent on student loans, they often offer students shoddy materials, cheap classroom conditions, and little instruction. Trade schools are sometimes unscrupulous, enrolling students in rapid-fire succession, taking their tuition up front, and discontinuing aid the second year when they were already on shaky ground but committed by debt. They also saddle students with huge debts that those students may not understand, operating as "cash machines for big banks," who pocket billions of dollars in guaranteed student loans and do not need to worry about checking students' credit. The government then has to pursue them to pay off their debts after they graduate and find that they are not qualified to hold the jobs they were promised. Hounded by collectors, many trade school graduates cannot even try school again because their defaults taint their credit.

Their defaults have become venom in the anti-student loan discourse, although it should have been clear to lenders from the beginning that many would never be able to repay those loans.

My son's friend Martin made mistakes in high school and, afterward, partying too much, floundered for his way. He suddenly joined the air force, relocated to North Dakota, and turned his life around. He earned a college degree, developed computer skills in logistics, cleaned up his credit, bought a Volkswagen Jetta, and has left enthusiastically for a posting in Germany with his wife and a new baby. When he comes back, he expects to get a GI loan to buy a house and to receive a good job in the private sector. His friends, struggling through college or looking for work, are dazzled by his apparent success.

Military recruiters have been quick to seize on students' increasing vulnerabilities as they face college and work. For example, the No Child Left Behind act quietly added military recruiters to an obscure provision requiring schools to release contact information for their students to certain outside agencies.[53]

For students who cannot afford college, the military is increasingly not just the best, but the only option. The army will pay up to $55,000 of your college loan (if you qualify and it's not in default). The basic benefit under the Montgomery GI Bill is that in return for contributing $100 per month for the first twelve months of active duty and serving for two years, a service member get $732 per month for up to thirty-six months or up to $28,800. If you enlist for three years or more, you get $900 per month for thirty-six months if you're a full-time student. Service members can also get tuition assistance for courses that they take while on active duty.[54]

Whatever disadvantages they have, student loans do offer students low interest and a long time to repay them. But the problem confronting higher education in this country is bigger than student loans: high tuition, surging debt, and increasingly unequal universities. Our taxes can be an investment in higher education, with repayment an educated and informed citizenry and opportunities for everyone. Despite the differences among them, students share the bad luck of a debtor generation.

In the summer of 2003, American University stopped accepting credit card payments for tuition, fee, and room and board charges. The fees that American paid credit card companies (not even counting the interest incurred by students) had approached $1 million per year.[55] And despite the befuddlement expressed by many students in the debt-poisoned university, many others have caught on. Some have come together to articulate the problems of debt in their lives, grasp connections, and redirect blame to banking and public policies, where it belongs. The United States Student Association has made student debt central to its political activities, and the

National Association of Graduate and Professional Students mobilized, largely through the Internet, to battle every program cut proposed by the *Contract with America*. University of Delaware students questioned MBNA's affinity card arrangement with the alumni association.[56] Students thus hold out hope that we can understand the role of debt in American life, that debt does not have to paralyze us, that private troubles *are* public issues, and that we can insist on more productive uses of our money. But first, we must follow creditors as they stalk their last prey: the poor.

Chapter 5

Pummeling the Poor

Will Harrison was a gifted designer, crafting exquisite compositions from living plants as well as the black and white silk flowers he arranged during our interview one Saturday morning. Born in 1945, he grew up on a small hog and vegetable farm on North Carolina's coastal plain. His parents, sisters, brother, and he worked as sharecroppers, rising before dawn each morning to strip and process tobacco from before he was "even tall enough to reach the leaves hanging from the ceiling." They earned $200 a year. He built up a healthy resentment of white landowners, but felt that these early lessons in working hard helped him work hard all his life. In the summer, kin and friends who had moved north sometimes returned "driving nice cars and wearing suits," and Harrison finally decided that "there must be something better than this." In 1961, along with his brother, cousins, and many other rural African Americans, he traveled to Washington to look for work in the expanding service sector. After staying briefly with his uncle, he lived in a series of apartments and worked at an array of restaurant jobs before encountering an established florist who took him on as an assistant, nurtured and disciplined the gifts that Harrison had cultivated as a farmer and then a gardener deft at wrestling stalwart greens, ruddy tomatoes, and lush grapes from the city soil.

Married twice, Harrison steered his two older children through a string of troubles. His oldest daughter struggles with different addictions. His son Kevin drove part time for Federal Express and did carpentry on the side before becoming disabled by AIDS. His third child completed college and has worked in television production, although her employment has been shaky because of the short life of new daytime shows. His wife, Mary, with whom he shared a small suburban house, works for the government. After the deaths of his uncles and his father, Harrison became even more central to a dispersed group of kin: his mother and brother (now back in North Carolina), his sisters in New York and Texas, and many cousins, mostly scattered around the Washington area. Harrison worked full-time, almost every day, with few vacations, for thirty-four years until both legs were amputated and he died of complications from diabetes. He once worked straight through the busy season with a dangerously swollen right leg, arguing, "I been hopping all this long, I can hop till after Mother's Day." Despite working hard, he was not able to make his business a success because of the debt peonage that stuck him with high interest and levels of insurmountable debt.

In 1991 Harrison's employer died, leaving the business to his wife. Feeling pinched, and lacking the loyalty her husband had felt toward Harrison, she slashed his salary from $15 to $7 an hour. Although his daughter had worked at after-school jobs (on an ice-cream truck, in McDonald's, and in a beauty parlor) since she was fourteen, and although Mary had a good job that included health insurance, he found that he could not support his suburban mortgage on this salary. Also, he was then forty-six. The salary seemed unjust and humiliating, and he decided to live out a longtime dream of starting his own business. Customers, friends, and family held his work in high regard; with his reputation, talent, and discipline for unrelenting work, his chances seemed good.

Harrison's only problem was that he lacked the capital to open a shop. His mother loaned him $10,000, all of her savings. He applied to several banks (including the one next door to his shop) and then to the government for a small business loan for minorities. He believed that his work history, residential stability, and plans to open a business in an underserved neighborhood would favorably dispose lenders toward his plans. However, he met repeated rejections as he sought to borrow $50,000. As he remembered it, he had to demonstrate that the flower shop would make $10,000 a month. He replied," I don't know if I can make $10,000 a year." Then, he reports, "The loan officer told me, 'You're better off trying to find you a nine to five job,' " a scenario Harrison saw as increasingly unlikely given the high unemployment rate and predominately low-wage service sector jobs available in Washington. "I'd rather be nine to five any day, and have a little time to myself. It's been three years and I haven't had a paycheck yet. No vacation. I told the guy I had to open the shop because I didn't have a job."

"Of course I had no problem getting a credit card, because that's money for the bank." In October 1991 Harrison opened his shop in a working-class African American neighborhood in suburban Maryland. He did so using credit cards, some newly acquired and others collected through the years. He charged a delivery van for $2,500 (which cost him many repairs and headaches), his counters, a refrigerator, and all of his supplies. He described an almost comical series of circuits to the cash advance machine on a Sunday to accumulate money for the deposit and first month's rent.

Harrison faced many of the difficulties inherent in small business, especially in the context of the brutal competition exacerbated by the entry of grocery store chains into mass marketing flowers: "You would be surprised at the florists in DC and Maryland, hundreds and hundreds, and the Chambers Funeral Home chain. The little florists can't compete with Giant and Safeway . . . they buy a whole tractor-trailer truckload and we have to buy it by the box. They say they're trying to make it convenient for the customers, the one-stop shop."

The flower business, like agriculture, is a seasonal enterprise. Most profits come during the Valentine's Day-Easter-Mother's Day ritual cycle, with the rest of the year lean and heavily reliant on funerals and weddings. For example, Harrison could count on doing $6,000 during the week before Mother's Day, but in the summer sales could plummet to $200 a week.

Harrison was also vulnerable to personal setbacks, spending six months in the hospital for blood clots in his legs induced in part by constant standing. He missed the crucial Valentine's Day crowd, relying on his wife, children, brother, and cousins to carry the shop. He said, "They did a hell of a job," but they had to work without an accomplished designer. However, Harrison's most serious problems lay in the debt he carried from starting the shop and, like a double-edged sword, the credit he had to offer customers to stay in business.

"The shop pays for itself, but I can't make the bills." Interest on his initial charges totaled $1,000 a month. When he became seriously delinquent, he visited a credit counseling service, which helped him consolidate his debts into one $900 per month payment to them, which was difficult to make in addition to his house note, the $3000 per month rent he paid for his shop, and hefty gas and electric bills of at least $500 per month from cooling and heating the large open space and refrigerating the flowers. At that point, determined to sever himself from consumer credit, he cut up all his cards and mailed them back. Still, he got cards in the mail, which he dutifully filed away: "I don't see why they go right on sending me more."

As a small merchant, Harrison was trapped from the seller's end of consumer credit as well. In many ways his shop harked back to an earlier mom-and-pop era or to the much-heralded family economy of immigrant shopkeepers. A local high school girl helped him out by copying items from a catalog onto index cards. His younger daughter worked there on school vacations and during summers; his son Kevin made deliveries during busy times; his older daughter, raising two children and receiving welfare, helped out several days a week, as did his first cousin. On the Saturday morning when I was last there, a woman and her niece came in to buy wedding runners. She had heard about Harrison because her father, who was getting married, lived in the same neighborhood as Harrison's brother-in-law: "I was so happy to hear there was a florist in this area." Several men popped in to chat and lingered to socialize. Despite the small town feel, though, a florist must also do business with strangers.

Harrison had to offer credit to be competitive, yet he could not afford the expensive technology that authorized credit at the point of purchase and thus lowered the risk of offering credit to customers he did not know. Many of his customers used credit cards, often by telephone, and especially on holidays. He sought authorization from Visa and MasterCard by telephone, but found that the companies did not always honor such authorizations. He showed me one example, when a customer charged a silk corn plant for $125 and a centerpiece for $65. He called it in: "They don't ask for no names, just our authorization number and the card number and expiration date. They don't say they're not going to be responsible till you send the money and it's not right." Harrison learned by telephoning the woman who had received the flowers that the customer was not the cardholder but a prisoner. When the Massachusetts cardholder signed a statement testifying that he had not made the purchase, the bank next door refused to pay the charge and deducted it from Harrison's account. (He hand-carried his charge slips to deposit there and they transferred the money into his account, but deducted it when it was not authorized.) In another example, a woman called in a charge for $99 worth of roses. Authorized by phone even though the Iowa cardholder was over the limit, Visa again refused to pay after the cardholder signed a statement denying the order. "They don't have to steal the card . . . they can be working at a place and see the number and just call it in."

Call-in problems were not the only ones Harrison had. Sometimes people simply signed the wrong name. And when he got busy, he made mistakes. One time he forgot to call in the charge until after the customer had left, and he was refused authorization. "This was my fault. He came and used a card. At the time I didn't call to authorize it, and they rejected it." He always tried to trace the buyers through the people who received the flowers, but "you can't charge them, they're not responsible." Even more important than fraud, however, were the multiple niggling fees, which escalated despite the "relationship banking" that he enjoyed with his bank next door. For example, his bounced check fees rose from $2 to $5 in two years, and, more importantly, yet inexplicably, so did his Merchant's Discount fees. When he opened the shop in October 1991 the rate was 3.45 percent. In January 1992 his statement simply announced that the fee was going up to 3.53 percent. In March it went up to 3.55 percent, and then to 4 percent. "They said it was because Visa and MasterCard (which always charge the same fee) had raised their processing fees."

How did Harrison survive and remain hopeful? In addition to working the long hours and drawing on the family resources that some Americans associate with immigrants, he developed at least one under-the-table strategy to save money. When customers paid in cash, he sometimes filed the

money in a drawer without ringing it up so that he could avoid the 5 percent sales tax. This stash helped him pay his credit card bills: for example
on one lucrative Mother's Day he earned the whole $900 payment for that
month. Harrison also loved his work and felt that his store anchored its
small shopping center, classed up the street, and acted as a force for good in
the community. By 1997, Harrison had spent more time in the hospital, lost
both legs, and begun a draining course of dialysis. His brother came up
from North Carolina to help Kevin close up the shop and auction off the
equipment.

Toward the end of his life, Will Harrison had a strong, clear sense of the
little injustices that had dogged his path and of how more equitable access
to credit might have boosted his chances. But from where he sat, he could
not piece it all together. Partly, this is because he blamed himself at the same
time that he felt ambivalent toward the banking companies.

Harrison's ambivalence and confusion also reflected vast political and
economic processes that reached far beyond his shop. He had a strong sense
of social justice and a keen consciousness of politics. He worried about Republican strategies to reduce social programs: "If they think crime is high
right now, just wait, because people are not going to let their children per-
ish." Although he struggled with racism all his life, he made many exceptions for white people whom he knew and trusted. Yet he felt hopeless about
social change, for the demonstrations and social movements of the 1950s
and 1960s did not appear to him to work anymore. Furthermore, like many
Americans, he found it difficult to link the clear posturing of the state to the
murky workings of credit and debt. Will Harrison's shop, and its neighborhood, pay dramatic witness to these larger forces at work as race intersects
place and debt drains resources and sucks capital away from more productive uses. Banks denied him money because they preferred high-interest
loans to more constructive and equitable investments. Their policies thus
propelled the inequality definitive of our time, denied Harrison a shot at his
dream, and left him remorseful, angry, and confused. And injustice hardens
into harsher inequality over time, as many black Americans discriminated
against in jobs, housing, and access to affordable credit have lacked the
wealth necessary to secure better futures for their children and grandchildren. His children have relied on the even more usurious fringe banks that
poor people have to use today, which in turn exacerbate inequality even
more.

In the second half of this chapter, I will look more closely at the fringe
banks in poor neighborhoods in order to contextualize Will Harrison's experiences and piece together the forces that left a hard-working and talented
man mired in debilitating illness and debt. Banking institutions rejected his
applications for affordable credit, and he was obliged to rely on usurious

credit cards as the only credit available in addition to the customary strategies used by the poor to mobilize kin. In Will Harrison's neighborhood, corporate finance capital (Fleet, Nations Bank, Citibank, Ford, and ITT) is
heavily implicated in fringe banking. Their storefronts are misleading, sig-
naling to poor customers that they belong, while masking the major role of
corporate finance, public trading, heavy investment, and heady profits.

A Crossroads of Race and Place

In 1990, banks entered the poverty debt market in earnest. This $5 billion
a year trade in financial services for the bankless makes Visa and Master-
Card seem, in the words of investigative journalist Mike Hudson, like
"kindly nonprofits." Their shift to high-interest, debt-generating businesses
topped off a forty-year decline in productive investment in cities, as capital
moved into suburban real estate and shopping malls, and industries moved
to the American South and then to other countries. Now, capital investment
has returned to cities as predatory lenders for the poor. The built environment illuminates these processes in many ways: in hulking, abandoned factories and poor communities where there are no jobs or banks. Affluent
neighborhoods and high-rent, tourist downtowns in many cities look like
those of Washington, D.C., where they teem with banks. But on South
Capitol Street in a poor neighborhood in the nation's capital, customers
sometimes stand twenty-deep in line at a tiny branch, and only *two* banks
serve one entire ward lying east of the Anacostia River. Fewer than nineteen banks operate in south central Los Angeles, which has as many residents as all of Washington. Ninety percent of the banks in the poorest
neighborhoods of Brooklyn and 20 percent of those in the Bronx have
closed since 1978.[1]

The neighborhood where Will Harrison tried to set up shop is littered
with pawnshops, rent-to-own centers, finance companies, check-cashing
outlets, and tax brokers offering rapid tax refunds. You can find such strips
in every American city, though each city's strips reflect the particular prob-
lems and possibilities of capital investment and abandonment there.
Louisville, Kentucky, sports many storefronts offering cash for houses. Mike
Hudson describes Roanoke, Virginia's, "Hall of Shame" featuring Credit
Tire and Audio, Mr. Car Man, Town and Country Pawn, Prime Time
Rentals, Avco Financial Services, Beneficial Finance, the Kar Korral, USA
Rents, the Automobile Exchange, and Bankers Optical. Adam Levy de-
scribes the intersection of Memorial and Columbia Drives in Atlanta,
Georgia,as a "haven for the shadow bankers." Saul Hansell evokes "Loan
Alley" in Nashville, and most readers will easily find them in poor and
working-class neighborhoods near or where they live.[2] These strips illumi-

nate the shackles that bind the poorest and most credit-damaged Americans to the wealthiest investors and largest corporations. The links reach from age-old mom and pop lenders through chain stores, corporate giants, and, like the bully's hulking big brother, Wall Street investors. The storefronts funnel the huge fees they charge the poor to the lives and projects of the wealthy.

"They Will Gladly Take a Check"[3]

Across the street from Will Harrison's shop lies a check-cashing outlet. It is a plain, grim storefront, staffed by one woman behind ceiling-high Plexiglas, offering pagers, laser tear gas, telephone calling cards, and myriad one-stop financial services. You can pay a bill, or "wire money in minutes worldwide" through an American Express MoneyGram. You can file a tax return and receive a rapid refund. ("After all . . . it's *your* money!" beams the promotional material.) You can pay gas, water, telephone, and electric bills, play the lottery ("We've got your ticket!"), and purchase money orders with the cash you receive when you cash your payroll, government, insurance, or tax refund check.

Customers must first become "members" for an initial fee and cool their heels while the staffer undertakes a thorough investigation by telephone. Customers at ACE sometimes feel humiliated and helpless, because the staffer snatches the check behind the Plexiglas before explaining what will happen. When asked how much it will cost, she gestures at the price list behind her, which is almost indecipherable. She then verifies the check by telephoning the party that issued it as well as the bank that backed it, identifying herself as a representative of Signet Bank. For the most routine checks, the outlet charges 2 percent of the total, but this varies quite a bit depending on the amount and type of the check and whether or not you have an ID. It can cost as much as 6 percent to cash a payroll check and 12 percent to cash a personal one.

The most outrageous, expensive, and quasi-legal transactions are called "payday loans," advances secured by a postdated personal check. Shops that specialize in payday loans have names like Check Into Cash, Check 'n Go, and Fast Cash. To borrow $100, a customer writes a check for $130 that the shop will cash when you get paid one or two weeks later. By Payday Loan Corporation's own reckoning, customers pay 1288.45 percent interest on five-day loans.[4] Sometimes customers bounce from one payday lender to another, borrowing from one to pay accumulating fees to the others.

By 1999 there were at least 8,000 payday loan shops and at least a dozen national chains. Nineteen states prohibit payday lending, but the other states and Washington, D.C., allow it. Some states specify a maximum fee of $15 for a one or two week loan of $100 or $200. Indiana limits the fee to $33, meaning that the annual percentage rate on a two-week loan would be 858 percent. These businesses escape scrutiny as they lend to the poorest borrowers, who are shunned by commercial banks as they seek small sums to get over a hump, fill a prescription, replace a tire, or celebrate Christmas. Payday loan practices seem designed to keep their customers in perpetual debt.[5]

Despite the shame, expense, and tedium of the process, many residents of poor neighborhoods conduct all their bankless business at places like America's Cash Express and Payday Loans. Even if there is a local bank, residents often cannot afford its minimum balance requirements, fees for checks, or high bounced-check penalties. Some residents do not have the major credit card that is needed to serve as a second major ID; some cannot manage a bank's restricted hours. Some people find banks discriminatory and insensitive. They may not have enough money in their account at the end of the month to cash a paycheck to pay their bills. They may need immediate cash to deliver to the telephone company in person. Some cannot open checking or savings accounts because of even minor problems with their credit or immigration histories. (Bad credit appears to have become such a marker of citizenship that poor people even find it hard to rent an apartment in many cities.)

Check-cashing outlets have blossomed in this harsh climate, with thousands operating nationally. The industry exploded in the 1980s and began to consolidate quickly in the 1990s. In 1993 check cashers cashed 150 million checks and charged $700 million in fees. In 1994 *Bank Marketing* magazine hailed Union Bank of San Francisco for pioneering check cashing services, proving that banks could find profits in poor neighborhoods. Bank vice president Yolanda Brown remarked, "Traditional thinking determines that low-income households represent low profit potential due to a small revenue base, high risk, and high cost of service. But if you shift the paradigm you find that financial services can be re-engineered, reinvented, repriced, and repackaged to meet legitimate demand at a significant profit."[6] Indeed.

Using check-cashing outlets further impoverishes and disenfranchises residents, leaving them with no records or proof of payment, no ongoing relationship to build up a credit history, and in greater personal danger from carrying cash (itself in jeopardy from fire, theft, or loss). From where they stand, residents may find it hard to connect the storefronts to the larger financial system or to the injustices they endure. Levy describes the views of

Atlanta snack food salesman Ronald Hayes, who makes a weekly visit to cash his $400 paycheck and buy a money order to pay a bill per week. The total cost is $15. "That's cheaper than belonging to a bank," claims Hayes, mistakenly embracing the outlets' misuse of the concept of "membership" as well as the fact that he is probably paying ten times more than a bank would charge. Even if they recognize the cost, others bow to hand-to-mouth demands for immediacy, safety, or convenience. One homeless man, coping successfully with the dangers of carrying cash, purchases a money order made out to himself each month, cashes it repeatedly at a 2 percent rate, and then buys another money order to carry the balance. He carries his money more safely but at a huge cost. Hudson interviewed two men in Manassas, Virginia, who paid $270 to cash a $4,500 insurance check because they didn't have time to wait for the check to clear. At the Eagle Outlet, where they cashed their check, owner Victor Daigle claimed that his customers "would rather pay a little bit more to us and have their convenience. They go to McDonald's because they want their hamburger right now. . . . They can come to us and get their money right now."[7] Daigle thus buys into mistaken ideas holding that the poor cannot defer gratification.

America's Cash Express's huge, colorful, block-lettered signs, modest exteriors, and familiar fast food floorplans promise false welcome to poor customers, while long waits, frustrated outbursts, and low-paid employees offer them little comfort. They also mask American Cash Express's close ties to large corporations and big banks. America's Cash Express is a national, publicly traded chain with sixty-nine outlets in the Washington area alone, and financial backing from American Express and Western Union, which opened its financial-services subsidiary, a "bank for the 'unbanked,'" after filing for bankruptcy in 1993 when new technology was devastating its once great telegram business.[8] The chain is growing so rapidly that it maintains a hotline to notify potential customers of new locations. It has displaced failing small stores, locally owned fringe banks, and, through the 1990s, even the smaller regional chains.

As banks have fallen to mergers and acquisitions, restructuring has led them to close less profitable branches and flee low-income neighborhoods where the primary business opportunities lie in low-profit retail banking. But they come right back in another guise: soaking the poor clients they abandoned through patriotic-sounding storefronts like America's Cash Express. Mostly unregulated, and protected by expensive lawyers, they reap profits from the devastation of the 1980s and, ultimately, make it worse. Only eleven states regulate check cashing. Douglas Merrill, director of the Georgia Check Cashers Association, argues, in yet another McDonald's analogy, "This is America. We don't order McDonald's to set the price of hamburgers.[9]

"THAT'S WHY THEY'RE MY CUSTOMERS"

Another, more venerable, fringe bank is the pawnshop, a familiar sight in cities for many years. Men in flop houses on Skid Row used to pawn their clothes for cash, and Elliot Liebow spotted one straightaway on Tally's Corner in 1963.[10] Pawn shops have proliferated in Washington, D.C., and the nation, doubling during the 1980s to number 10,091 in 1994, and between 13,000 and 15,000 by 2002. Most of the large chains are based in Texas. On their website, First Cash Financial Services touts: "Texas isn't just oil, land, and cattle fortunes. Since the 1980s, a new industry has found a home on the range: Pawn shops."[11] Pawnshops have become centralized and are backed by upscale marketing, ruthless acquisitions, and persistent pressure on state governments to raise usury rates. Like check-cashing outlets, they displace small businesses, family-owned pawnshops, and local chains, and, like other fringe banks, offer low-paying jobs. Unfortunately, they do not offer benefits or a living wage.

Cash America, founded in 1983, operates hundreds of pawnshops in the United States, England, and Sweden. It has bought up a string of little shops.[12] One of five chains to be publicly traded, it boasts PWN (for pawn) as its symbol, turns lush profits for investors, and has tried to upgrade the pawnshop image as it eyes markets all over the world. Cash America was the first and largest of a new wave of modern chains that consolidated this old industry and tried to spruce up its cramped and dingy image. Its visionaries "saw the industry as ripe for a revolution, inspired by a sagging economy, a rash of personal bankruptcies and a growing segment of the population that had bad credit and limited access to the banking industry.[13] If you multiply its monthly rate by 12, its annual interest rate hovers at around 200 percent, not unusual in an industry that often charges 240 percent. NationsBank, which holds $157 billion in assets and racks up good will with its self-publicizing community development programs, neglects to trumpet the $175 million line of credit it extended to Cash America in 1993 to expand its shops. In Washington, D.C., we might even see a giant like Cash America merge with or acquire the relatively small but enormously successful Famous Pawn, which is preparing the way by gobbling up mom-and-pop stores in poor neighborhoods.

Famous Pawn began with one storefront in the small shopping center where Will Harrison struggled to sell flowers. During his time there, the pawnshop oozed closer and closer, so that now it occupies the spaces of four stores. Staffers stand behind floor-to-ceiling Plexiglas to greet customers. The store is stuffed with former collateral for these expensive secured loans: gold chains, wedding bands, watches, baseball cards, leather jackets, computers, VCRs, television sets, compact discs, cameras, pianos, guitars, saxophones, power tools, lawnmowers, and cars. Like all pawnshops, it is filled with stories of failed dreams, broken lives, and desperate, last-ditch grabs for cash. From Chicago, Steve Mills writes, "But the musical instruments, electronics equipment, and jewelry do carry with them stories of bad luck and heartbreak, misfortune and need—musicians waiting for the next gig, shoppers deep in debt, lovers who no longer look fondly on their gifts."[14]

Customers pawn these items for 10 percent interest each month, a relatively low rate set by Maryland and the District. A borrower would receive $100 for a pawned item and redeem it in thirty days for $110.00. They usually pay the borrower $.25 for every dollar of its value. One customer complains, "They don't give you nothin' for it. But when they sell it, that's when they mark it up." If a customer is unable to redeem it then, the shop will keep it on hold for as long as you can pay each month's interest. Often, pawn shop profits lie in nurturing these long-term relations with borrowers, who come in to pay their "dues" on the first of each month, but sometimes give up and let their treasures go. Their misfortune allows Famous Pawn to bulge out of its space, overflowing with pawns, featuring a long line of borrowers every day, and swallowing its neighboring establishments. Secondary buyers cruise through periodically, buying up items in bulk and boosting profits in the retail side of the business, which has long been less profitable than the interest-collecting side.

Most neighborhood residents pawn rather than buy, although pawnshops offer the only shopping opportunities here. One man worries about the trend, "They're like McDonald's, springing up all over. Whenever a store closes down, a pawn shop takes its place." He believes that some, but not all of the goods are stolen, because pawnshops provide a rare source of cash in this capital-starved neighborhood. "I won't even buy a VCR," he explains, "because it's just an invitation to steal." Although the shop staff is supposed to record a borrower's address from a driver's license, this man feels that kids often steal the goods and ask a friendly adult to pawn them.

People go to pawnshops so that they can buy food, pay bills and rent, fix the car, visit a clinic, fund birthdays, or try new ventures. Some pawn to stretch out cash until payday. One man pawns his bicycle regularly each month for ten days and redeems it when he is paid. Will Harrison' son, Kevin, has pawned everything that he owns, including his sofa, a bedroom suite, and hard-earned carpentry and plumbing tools. He pays interest each month on a small collection of baseball cards that he found during a repair job, in the hope that they will be a nest egg for his daughter. Steve Krupnik, president of the Indiana Pawnbrokers Association, says "It's the only place where you can borrow money and they won't ruin your credit, we don't make your life miserable, and you can still come back and borrow again."[15]

Borrowers, like buyers, are increasingly diverse, as formerly middle-class people suffer layoffs, bankruptcies, foreclosures, medical debt, widowhood and divorce. Levy met expensively dressed Tony Lawrence at EZ Pawn in Atlanta, toting a Yamaha stereo receiver and a Fisher amplifier. "I have a bank account and credit cards," Lawrence explained. "But I'm maxed out on those." A pawnbroker in Florida told Levy that he had recently loaned $2,000 to a small business owner in exchange for his gold Rolex watch so that the businessman could meet his payroll!

But the vast majority of borrowers are poor, with incomes between $9,000 and $17,000 a year, according to John Caskey. They are young, in and out of work, and disproportionately of color. Cash America's *Annual Report* describes them this way: "The cash-only individual makes up the backbone of America. He's the hard-working next door neighbor, the guy at the corner service station, or the lady who works as a checker at the local supermarket." Caskey quotes Jack Daugherty of Cash America to some-what different effect: "I could take my customers and put them on a bus and drive them down to a bank and the bank would laugh at them. That's why they're my customers."[16]

"AND YOU DON'T NEED CREDIT TO GET IT"

Late at night, or midafternoon during the judge shows, if you turn on the television, you will find a barrage of commercials inviting you to rent to own. A middle-aged white woman asks, "If somebody goes to work every day and they have bad credit or no credit, there's really no reason why (they) shouldn't be able to have nice things. With Rent-A-Center you can." And a Latina in her early twenties claims, "For what it cost me at the Laundromat, I got a washer/dryer at Rent-A-Center. . . . And you don't need credit to get it!" (Sometimes these advertisements urge you not to steal, but try a Pay-day Loan, or liken your checking account to an empty, dribbling bottle of ketchup.)

Rent-to-own stores emerged to evade usury laws limiting the interest paid by people who bought appliances and furniture on credit, by redefining what they were doing as renting. Their profits stem from astounding markups, or interest, as customers often pay five times what they would for retail purchases of the same items. For example, if you bought a nineteen-inch television in Washington, D.C. in 1997, you would have paid $7.00 a week for seventy-eight weeks. The television would have cost you $546, or $226 more than you would have paid in a retail store. This amounts to interest of about 150 percent. If you had bought a refrigerator in Atlanta that year, you would have paid $20 a week for seventy-four weeks for a total cost of $1500. In a regular store, the refrigerator would have cost about $880.[17] You paid an extra $620 for the refrigerator in about eighteen months, about 400 percent interest.

The largest rent-to-own operator is Rent-A-Center, with 29 percent of the share of this market. Rent-A-Center began with eight stores in 1986 and grew quickly through a long string of acquisitions. The entire industry has grown steadily since its beginning, but Rent-A-Center has been especially fast. In 1999 Wall-Street.com chose Rent-A-Center for its Fast-Growing Companies list, which included those 15 percent of American companies noted for "exceptional long-term sales growth, recent growth trends, size and stock price.[18] In 2003 Rent-A-Center owned 2,567 stores nationwide. It was incorporated in Delaware, but its headquarters lies in Plano, Texas. In 2003 the company earned profits of about $100 million despite settling in a class-action gender discrimination lawsuit by female employees and applicants.[19]

To walk into Rent-A-Center on Georgia Avenue in Washington, D.C., is to discover a lush cornucopia of household consumer goods: florid bedroom furniture; leather couches; brightly colored, blaring television sets; giant, gleaming refrigerators; and shimmering gold jewelry. The store offers impoverished customers a shot at the postwar American dream. But the giddy interior, slick brochures, and the convenience (or urgency?) of instant purchases and free delivery belie Rent-A-Center's harsh and greedy terms. To qualify, applicants must fill in boxes privileging "Government Financial Assistance Information" and provide the names and addresses of six references, two of whom must be relatives. Consumer groups have targeted rent-to-own stores for shoddy sales practices, shady tack-on fees, abrupt, humiliating collections, and all manner of harassment and psychological torture.[20]

A Festival of Debt

In the 1990s, banks hawking secured credit cards set up booths beside vendors selling African folk art and Asian jewelry or grilling pupusas and steaming tamales at multicultural street festivals. Secured cards ranged into what was then a new market, composed of people who are too poor, or whose credit histories are too shaky, to qualify for ordinary credit cards. Marketed by mail and 900 telephone numbers to people with poor credit, or through radio and television spots, newspapers, and magazines, and in stores, fringe banks, and carryouts throughout working-class neighborhoods, their invasion of festivals celebrating diversity and community is particularly galling.

A secured card works like this: you open a savings account with a bank for a relatively small amount (usually several hundred dollars) and receive a bankcard with a credit line equal to between 50–100 percent of your savings account balance. Usually you pay a processing fee with your application, relinquish access to your funds as long as your credit card account is open, and agree to allow the bank to apply your savings to your credit card balance "in case of default." You make monthly payments on your credit card account and send in additional savings deposits whenever you want to increase your credit line. If your balance is paid in full, you may close your credit card account and receive your savings back, but only after forty-five days so that all charges can clear. Building or repairing credit appears to be a prime incentive, and banks purposefully sought people with poor enough credit that they would be willing to pay high interest. For example, Bank-First in South Dakota has founded what it calls the "American Fair Credit Association," so that its "members" can restore their creditworthiness through secured cards. Promotional materials say nothing about high annual fees ranging from $20 to $75, low, even no interest paid on your savings account, or the credit card interest rates that run as high as 22 percent. "Basically, you're lending someone back their own money and charging them a lot of money for it," Chicago financial services consultant John M. Stein told Suzanne Wooley.[21]

Secured cards are controversial even within the industry. Some find it distasteful to work from lists of people with bad credit. Others believe that "trading of derogatory information is permissible if it results in a useful offer." The Federal Trade Commission has wondered if it is even legal. Some bankers worry about contaminating their image through sleazy television commercials and 900 numbers, which might result in short-term profits from telephone charges and application fees but damage a bank "seeking long-term profitability by the development of their card portfolios."

However, other analysts argue that "banks can make rich profits from poor credits", "for banks able to manage the process, battered consumer balance sheets may turn out to be a gold mine." On an outstanding balance of $1,000, a bank offering a card with an 18 percent rate and paying 5 percent on a cardholder's deposit can make a 5 to 7 percent after-tax return. With interest rates today significantly lower than this, the profit is greater. The bank's risks are quite small, because the loan is collateralized, and if secured cardholders do manage to build a credit history, they might remain loyal to the bank that got them started.

Although pioneered by Key Federal Savings and Loan in 1982, the major credit card issuers generally ignored this market niche until the late 1980s. In the 1990s, however, secured cards were among the most profitable segments of the credit card portfolio, due to high interest rates, lack of defaults, and annual fees. Citibank was the industry leader in these accounts, which it recruited largely from its own "turndown list."[22]

Other, newer companies, like Orchard Bank and Aspire, specialize in people with terrible credit, offering very low loans and huge fees for paying late or going over your limit, where you might be propelled into further debt by the cost of the fees themselves. Still other companies (such as First National Merchants) offer credit cards that allow only catalog shopping (in the company's own catalog) and "hassle-free fast cash" in amounts from $20 to $150. First National piles on membership activation fees ($200), annual fees ($99) and cash available fees. Like lawyers who haunt courthouses to follow court cases on garnishment, repossession, eviction, and foreclosure, these card issuers prey on the credit-damaged fallout of those who generate debt.

Luis's Story

Luis Perez grew up with his mother in a small apartment. Ms. Perez, born in Guatemala, is a domestic worker who works about twelve hours a day covering as many houses as she can. Often on his own as a teenager, Luis hung out at a local restaurant, where he developed a close relationship with a cook and sometimes worked as a bus boy. "It was basically a get 'em off the street kind of job," he says. When he graduated from high school, he began working two jobs, installing cable television in the day and ushering in a movie theater at night. He was not able to earn enough to buy a car or a house, but he was able to rent a small apartment. Because he had trouble paying his bills, he decided to pursue his dream of becoming a wrestler. After expensive training in Florida, taken on because the promoter promised him that he could wrestle professionally in the Caribbean, he applied for his first credit card at the age of twenty-five. He received a 24 percent interest secured card from Key Federal Bank, but when the wrestling promises proved bogus, he quickly became too indebted to pay his minimum and now dodges his creditors as best he can, while working double shifts as a waiter to try to accumulate enough money to pay his rent and his debts. Their dunning letters to him began with phrasing such as the following:

Dear Luis,

    Allow me to introduce myself. My name is Joan and my job at Key Federal is to contact cardholders, such as yourself, who may be experiencing difficulty in meeting their monthly payment obligations. . . . I have found that once an avenue of communication has been established, most problems are easily resolved. . . . I sincerely believe that together we can work this problem out and put your account back on the right track.

They now sound more like this:

[No greeting] *Your account is now delinquent in the amount of $40.00.* Until your account is current and below your established credit line, we must insist you do not use your card. We must also inform you that failure to make at least the minimum monthly payment will leave us no other alternative but to turn your account over to our Collection Attorneys. Please be advised your account is also being reported as delinquent to a local credit bureau.

KEY FEDERAL SAVINGS BANK

Luis says that he uses his credit cards for Christmas, food, and beer. "I waste a lot on friends. It makes you more generous. I buy rounds of drinks. I give cash to friends." He also uses the ATM for walking-around money. Sometimes "I use it 3 or 4 times a day—getting $10-$10-$10-$10. I try to hold back and only spend that amount. If your card is rejected, they charge you ten to fifteen bucks, something like that. And they never explain it to you."

My beef is I went to Atlanta. I had just gotten the card, only had it for two days. I go to use it and see if it works. I got a CD—it worked—I rented a car and it worked. OK they keep working until I get to the airport and they say, "Sorry you don't have enough for a ticket. Call this 800 number." So I called the number and it was closed for the weekend. I said, "No, you have to help me. What's the deal? I should have $600."

Luis also pawns—a lot.

I've pawned my boom box, my speakers, a real nice ring. Once I needed money on short notice to go to Guatemala. I pawned a really expensive ring, and a brand new gun, never fired. They gave me $300. They catch people in debt or [people] who need something they shouldn't need it for. A lot of that stuff looks too good—the VCRs look brand spanking new, fur coats, leather jackets.

He also goes to check-cashing joints:

I've been to those a lot. I used to be a member of ACE at 18th and Florida. There's no point in having a bank account. You have to go to ACE while the banks are still open, they call the bank, give you a card with your name on it.

He relies on friends. When we talked, he was assembling a Volkswagen Bug, using lots of help from friends whom he would repay by working off the debt. "By the time I'm finished, it will be lots cheaper than a new car. A maximum of $4000, but it won't be that."

But Luis believes that in the long run

a credit card's the thing. You go to a video store, you can't join up unless you have a credit card. It's ridiculous, outrageous. Mine expired. I said, "I've been coming here for the longest time." They said, "It's policy. Bring a credit card number." When I was younger, you shake my hand, I trust you. I don't trust people anymore.

Poor neighborhoods teem with other high-profit, debt-generating schemes, including income tax refund anticipation loans. Using confusing, deceptive advertising, such as Rapid Refunds, SuperFast Cash, Instant Money, Fast Cash Refunds, these loans prey on the poorest, most cash-strapped taxpayers. Borrowers may not even realize that rapid refunds are loans because they are marketed as quick electronic returns, helpful to people with emergency needs and without up-front cash to pay tax preparation fees. These borrowers pay from $29 to $89 for loans that last about ten days, paying interest rates of about 774 percent in 2002. Often, those who borrow are eligible for the Earned Income Tax Credit, but they do not have money up front for tax preparation fees.[23] The loans are not regulated by the state or the federal government and in fact are encouraged by the IRS goal to stimulate electronic filing.

Tax returns often mark a time of ready cash in poor neighborhoods, and predators move in to take a cut. Rent-A-Center notes, for example, "Historically, we have seen greater cash sales and more frequent exercises of early purchase options in the first quarter of the year as our customers receive their income tax refunds."[24]

MELISSA'S STORY

Poor people also lease money. In 1996, Melissa Peters, a young black woman, described her experience leasing cash this way:

I was in a bind. I remembered hearing an advertisement over the radio station that I listen to which announced "$200 cash in minutes." The telephone number was also easy to remember: 301–702–CASH. I decided to call. "Well, Miss Peters, based on what you have told me thus far, you qualify for our services. Just bring to our office the following items: the first sheet of your telephone bill, a current paystub, two checks, a driver's license, the makes, models, and serial numbers of the two appliances that you own and we'll have $200.00 cash in your hands in minutes!" She [the lender] went over the sales leaseback agreement very quickly, stating that she could cash the $200 check at the bank located on the first floor if she hurried. The agreement works like this. The term is fifteen days; the two appliances that the customer has listed on the agreement are given a fair market value of $100 per item; the appliances are now the property of the company and the customer is renting this property for $2 per item per day. The customer has several options when paying off the debt: after fifteen days, the customer can pay off the debt in full at $270 (35 percent more than the customer received); after fifteen days, the customer can pay off one item at $165 and have another fifteen days to pay off the second item at $135 (50 percent more than the customer received); after fifteen days, the customer can pay for the rental only—$60–and then must go back to the first option.

Many other schemes involve opportunities to sell or rent you cars and car accessories, and then take them back. In Virginia, customers can find stores like Roanoke's Credit Tire and Audio (for tires and car stereo systems), rent-to-own cars, and transmission jobs on credit. Washington's Metro buses carry cards for riders wishing to apply for E-Z Auto Loans. Despite the lure of 0 percent financing, car loans in poor neighborhoods go for 20 to 30 percent interest, especially designed for people with bad credit. Many cities offer car-title pawns, where the title to the car serves as collateral for a high-interest loan with an interest rate of up to 1000 percent. "Second-Chance" auto financing operations require expensive warranties, insurance, and 50 percent interest. Hudson notes that these are often "churning operations," because businesses sell a car, collect the down payment and a few installments, then repossess and resell it.[25] One African American woman described her son's experience with cars in the 1990s in Louisville, Kentucky, like this:

When Rico started to drive, my father told him absolutely no more cars unless the grades and responsibility level improved. He found all these pay on the lot car dealers, and it seems to me that he bought at least four like this until he went into the Navy! They were not checking his credit and did not even check for insurance or even if he had a driver's license! He would buy a car, pay for it a couple of weeks—yes you can buy a used car and pay for it weekly in this underground market!—then something would go wrong with the car . . . *or* he would get stopped by the cops for driving without a license and/or insurance . . . *or* he would wreck the car and then get in trouble because [he had] no license and or insurance . . . then as soon as that incident was taken care of (usually entailing legal fees due to no license and/or insurance, fixing car, or dumping car—I did this so many times I can't count) . . . and a couple of months later he had talked some used car dealer (ad states that they *finance on the lot*) into getting another auto. These guys apparently never checked his references because sometimes he had a job and they were never, at any rate, full time . . . and they were getting the money every week and charging all kinds of interest and fees . . . when the incident occurred at Columbine and I saw all of those new model autos in that student parking lot, and the newscasters kept stating that this was an upper middle-class area, I thought there is another story here that should be told!

"OUR DREAM WAS TO BUY A HOME"

In 1993, Lowell Spencer reported to Congressman Joseph Kennedy's Subcommittee on Consumer Credit and Insurance of the House Banking Committee:

I am originally from Jamaica and I came to this country in 1973. I have worked for the Brooklyn Hospital for over 15 years. Our dream was to buy a home. We had tried several times but never accomplished our goal. . . . Approximately two months ago, I applied for a mortgage with Chemical Bank. The branch manager told me that my application was quite favorable and that I should get some good news in about four days. My credit was not perfect but it was not bad. I always paid my bills, I had a steady job and my wife also works for the Brooklyn Hospital with good incomes. Since we had been approved for a mortgage a year ago I felt confidant [sic]. Four days passed and I called the branch manager. He told me "confidentially" that the mortgage application was denied. I was shocked and disappointed because I thought that after twenty years in this country my dream of buying a home was in my grasp . . . my application was denied because I didn't have enough money for closing costs, which was not true![26]

During the early 1990s, leading newspapers thoroughly reported discriminatory practices by mainstream banks in offering what Americans widely regard as "good debt." For example, the 1991 Boston Federal Reserve Board study on mortgage and home equity loans documented much higher rejection rates for African and Latin Americans at all income levels, paralleling known discrimination by secondary lenders nationally and in Washington, D.C.

In the District of Columbia, black applicants were rejected at double the rate of whites in 1991, with one-third of all black applicants rejected for mortgages and even well to do black applicants turned down 23.2 percent of the time. Despite the publication of these results, it happened again in 1992, when the situation appeared to have grown even worse, and again in 1993: Black and Latino applicants were still twice as likely to be rejected, with loans to white neighborhoods approved at twice the rate as loans to black neighborhoods.

Several banking policies undergirded this discrimination: the dated evaluation system that certifies a narrow slice of Americans who are white, middle-class, and use banks; the abandonment of branches in unprofitable neighborhoods; the failure of banks to develop good working relationships with black realtors; a reluctance to fund mortgages deemed too low to be profitable; and an unwillingness to lend money for semidetached houses or to finance mortgages in neighborhoods where more than half the units are rented.

These national mortgage trends had sinister implications. The house is the main source of equity for those working-class people fortunate enough to have squeezed into the racially subsidized housing market of the 1950s and 1960s. Restrictive covenants constrained white homeowners from selling to members of many different minority groups. Breaking into all-white neighborhoods often involved expensive, trying, and perilous blockbusting in the wake of white flight. After the ravages of the 1980s, the house may have become one's only wealth to pass on to the next generation, members of which are increasingly unable to buy houses.

When banks fail to lend in minority neighborhoods, they contribute to deterioration and reinforce the downward economic spiral in several ways. Houses may sit on the market longer, reducing neighborhood demand, and offering easy prey to speculators. Loan denials ripple through the housing market, exacerbating the effectiveness of historic restrictive covenants and redlining, the blight inflicted by capital abandonment, the unavailability of affordable housing, new restrictions on public housing units that demand perfect credit, and the difficulty people find in renting without good credit.

One exception was mobile homes. Between 1991 and 1998 the annual sales of manufactured mobile homes tripled in number to 374,000. Green Tree Financial financed more than 40 percent of them, lending to borrowers with little chance of paying them back. Green Tree, by then Conseco, repossessed twenty-five thousand trailer homes in 2001 alone.[27]

After the 1986 laws offering tax breaks for a second mortgage, discrimination in housing in poor neighborhoods took a new form, a kind of reverse redlining. Finance companies began to peddle loans to people who were financially desperate or credit starved and who needed to consolidate debt or make home repairs. These firms targeted minority, fixed- or low-income, low-wage, or Social Security-dependent households that often held substantial equity in their homes as their sole investment. Not surprisingly, lenders charge high interest. They tack on worthless, expensive "credit insurance." They pursue ruthless, haranguing collection policies. Sometimes they refinance, or "flip," these loans several times, piling on fees along the way: prepayment penalty fees, more credit insurance, and loan origination fees. All the fees are also financed at high interest. The customer may be left with shoddy repair work, a huge debt, the threat of foreclosure, and nobody to hold responsible.[28]

Reverend Charles Green, president of Roanoke's NAACP, told Mike

Hudson, "I don't guess that a week goes by that I don't get something in the mail from somebody who wants to give me a second-mortgage loan on my home—just because of my address." In offering mortgages and home equity loans, once again, alternative institutions replace mainstream banks. Mortgage companies, and their staff, working entirely on commission, fax and pepper minority neighborhoods with lending opportunities, trolling for high interest loans.

In Washington, D.C., Monument Mortgage advertises in the *District Merchandiser*, flaunting a photograph of its African-American "senior loan officer." It offers potential applicants a checklist that includes "No Savings," "Bankruptcy," "Looming Foreclosure," "Too Much High Interest Debt," and "Kid in College." Monument also offers same-day appraisals, one-week approvals: "Bad Credit O.K." "We specialize in bad credit. . . . Our "multiple sources of funds permits more creative and flexible loans." Indeed. Because they do not collect deposits they are not bound by the Federal Depositors Insurance Corporation regulations. So the largest banks set up subprime subsidiaries to take advantage of that. They can charge whatever they want. Washington, D.C., like other places, does not place interest caps on mortgage loans. The 24 percent cap on a second mortgage is virtually unregulated given current low interest rates. In 1996, KeyCorp, the nation's eighth largest bank, announced it would just become a financial services company instead of a bank. Key fired 2,700 employees and went on a buying spree to dominate the subprime market.

Front-line loan sharks like United Companies Financial Corporation of Louisiana, Capital City Mortgage Corporation in Washington, and Delta funding in Brooklyn funnel money from poor neighborhoods through big players like Chase Chemical Bank, Fleet Financial Corps of New England, Ford (whose financial service associates may keep it afloat), General Electric (the largest of all through its Capital Services unit), BankAmerica (through its Security Pacific division), General Motors, Westinghouse, Bankers Trust Company, Chase Manhattan, Norwest, NationsBank (after it acquired ChryslerFirst), KeyCorp, Countrywide Credit Industries, Transamerica, and Continental Grain through ContiFinancial. Bankers provide the initial cash to make the loans, pull together layers of financial and insurance companies, and bundle the loans into mortgage-backed securities to sell on Wall Street. Wall Street adds brand-name respectability and sophisticated advertising and obscene profits. Investors and bankers so distance themselves from the people who hawk the loan that sometimes the company you think loaned you the money is really just servicing it. They sell pools of loans to institutional investors like pension plans and universities, and it's hard for these investors to know where the funds come from. It's all like a glorified money-laundering operation, with lots of risks and rewards.[29]

In the 1990s the market in mortgage-backed securities grew from 9 billion to 140 billion. The poverty business is very good. "This [United] is one cheap growth stock," said financial analyst Stephen Eisman to reporter Michael Quint. He noted that demand for United's subprime loans was little affected by rising interest rates and said the company could earn $5.75 a share next year, up 26 percent from 1994.[30] These subprime loans (which refer to the customer, not the interest rate) go to the captive market of people with no credit history, or a tarnished one. Lenders prey on desperate, depressed, delusional, elderly, illiterate, incarcerated, regular people who may have children or who need bail or tuition or who seek funds for a medical emergency. People who need cash for their houses become permanent income streams for the lender. This flow of money from the poor to the rich is just one example of how middle- and upper-class economic privileges are sustained by the poor, who participate, expensively and extensively, in the cycle of debt that has become the primary mechanism of American economic wealth growth.

As it did in the 1970s when credit cards first captured its attention, Congress responded to this new predatory lending frenzy by mandating more disclosure. In 1994 Congress expanded federal truth-in-lending rules so that predatory lenders had to give more information: what one's monthly payments will be, the exact interest rate, and the risk of losing one's home. But it has not been enough.

Foreclosures on homes hit thirty-year highs nationally in 2002; foreclosures in Louisville, Kentucky, more than doubled from 437 in 1996 to 982 in 2000. Sometimes these foreclosures abet gentrification. For example, in the summer of 2003, houses in Washington, D.C.'s Petworth neighborhood fell like dominoes, as longtime African American owners borrowed money on their houses and lost their homes, which were snatched up quickly by speculators and new residents.

For years, American ethnographies have disclosed deep, broad social networks of sharing and pooling among people who are poor. Poor people often cope with poverty by distributing money, food, supplies, housing, favors, and child care along the axes of the friendship and kinship networks that sustain poor households. Poor peoples' networks are often both flexible and strong; they connect people intergenerationally and through time across households.[31]

Today, everyday credit and debt through which people aid and obligate friends and allies and manage crisis operates in the context of debt they incur in more oppressive relationships, tethering people to costly obligations and onerous penalties in exchange for urgently needed cash. How have these new debt-generating institutions affected the life of poor communities? How do residents of poor neighborhoods survive, maneuvering in a deteriorating labor market, often living on a cash-only basis, assaulted by predatory lenders, media, and the state?

I explore these assaults below, illustrating them with the experiences of some poor people in Washington, D.C. Every city has experienced a different kind of job loss. Some have witnessed the flight of industrial jobs overseas. In 2003 North Carolina was devastated by the flight of its long-sustaining textile industry. Buffalo lost its call centers. Washington, D.C. has suffered from the decline of public sector jobs and the rise of freelancing, commissioned, tip-driven jobs. In 2003 the unemployment rate was stuck at 31.6 percent for young black men, and this figure included only those men who were still actively looking for work. Their options were severely limited. Capital One sought people to work from home collecting judgments. You could even garnish wages after you learned how, but you first had to buy a package containing an instruction manual, a diskette, and the proper forms, for $149.99.[32]

Some people resort to the drug business, sometimes in the hope of helping their families, sometimes in the desire to raise enough money to start a small business. Some must overrely on the informal economy: lining up early in the morning, hugging their power tools, at pick-up locations; taking on sporadic part-time, seasonal, and day labor employment at construction sites, sporting events, and cultural festivals; selling antibiotics, weed, guns, or sex; freelancing in plumbing, painting, landscaping, carpentry, baby sitting, gypsy cabs, car maintenance, and masonry; setting up informal street markets for buying and selling clothes, videotapes, VCRs, antiques, and beepers; scavenging, spot work, off-the-books work, recycling.[33]

People devise many other ways to get cash: they sell food, food stamps, or bootleg liquor on Sundays. They watch parked cars. Young women do hair. Participating in focus groups, surveys, and other studies brings in extra cash. Equipment is precious: you can tape movies in the theater and repackage them for sale as videos while the film is still on the big screen; with a car you can offer people rides home from the bus station or the grocery store; a lawn mower empowers a grass-cutter, a set of tools a mechanic. The pawnshops bursting with power tools that surround Washington, D.C. testify to the frequency with which these strategies fail. Poor people today often survive through a virtual family economy that depends on lots of labor to package enough income to sustain itself. Small children may be sent out to carry groceries at the Safeway or walk dogs. People with AIDS have access to extra resources: food, medicines, checks to spend at Safeway, housing vouchers, and legal aid. They package income from friends, relatives, the market, and the state, thus meeting daily subsistence requirements most of the time. But crises recur often: illness, rent hikes, heating failure, eviction; expected expenses like new shoes or winter coats for children; unexpected expenses like school trips, illness, complications in pregnancy, telephone or utility disconnection.

Kevin is the son, now 40, of Will Harrison. His story is a tragic account of waste and triage. Mostly his father raised him and his sister after his parents divorced. He was jailed at nineteen for armed robbery. He did well in jail, buying cigarettes cheap and selling them singly and becoming the baker so he could control the supply of yeast. When he got out ten years later, he worked with his uncle doing electrical work, on his own as a carpenter, and part-time as a driver for UPS. His handiness made him unusual. He devoted a lot of time and thought figuring out how things work, and he could fix or build seemingly anything. Kevin had cash problems all the time, and he became adept at pawning. I went with him one day to his most-trusted shop, King Pawn, where he had pawned everything of value he owned, including all his expensive tools. He married and had a daughter, the light of his life. But he couldn't seem to stay out of trouble, especially after being diagnosed with AIDS. With AIDS, he was eligible for certain kinds of private and public help. He got food stamps, bus and subway tokens, a bag of groceries every week, and many kinds of medicines. He soon grew deft in selling and trading all of these supplies. In the summer of 2001, after splitting with his wife, he wrote down part of his story for me.

KEVIN'S STORY

When I met Cheryl, she was in the street with nothing. Something about her attracted me. She was what you call strung out. At that time I was out there too. And we ended up talking. Shortly after that she started living with me at my mother's house; Cheryl and Letitia [her daughter]. My mother ended up putting us both out for smoking crack cocaine, it was hard to manage having two drug addicts, so I proceeded trying to find somewhere for us to live and sleep. My grandmother let us live with her awhile. She really tried to help. Then when time ran up at Grandmother's I told a friend of mine that I needed a place to stay. He said, "Cool." Then I said, "But I have my girlfriend and her daughter with me." He said, "Let me talk to Moms." They took us all in, Cheryl, Letitia, and me.

This person I have become wasn't all my doing, because if you get the big picture, meaning anyone, I truly in my heart understand that I have been devastated. My father died and then about a few months later I was diagnosed with full blown AIDS. . . . I tried. I threw in the towel on myself. My daughter helped me to be able to deal with what I went through. I thought I was doing such a great job, you couldn't tell me I wasn't the world's best dad. I wasn't able to work due to my illness. But I did all the shopping, cooking, cleaning, car repairs, house repairs, and childcare.

While being down in North Carolina it gave me a chance to think about how far I had come. From being a troubled child to trying to raise a child myself. When I returned to Washington [D.C.], after finding out that I had a warrant for my arrest, I was shocked about the charges. A very bad picture was painted of me. I'm not and don't try to be a criminal. I feel it to be unfair to allow Cheryl to do this to me. I don't want trouble. I want peace. I learned my lesson years ago. I've been punished enough. I didn't go looking for trouble. Trouble came after me.

Kevin comes from a huge, closely knit extended family ranging from North Carolina through Washington to New York. He has helped them, and leaned on them, during his entire life. He and his cousins spent his summers at the home of his grandparents when they were children. His uncle there taught him to fish, cook, garden, and repair things. When he first got out of jail, his older cousin found him kitchen work. Some of his relatives have died, and most are strapped. Perhaps the most tragic part of his story is that the others have triaged him. He has caused them too much trouble over the years, and they cannot cope with him anymore. Ever resilient, however, Kevin met a woman in Benton Harbor, Michigan, who supports herself and her daughter on disability, and he moved in with them. He tries to make amends and repair hard feelings with his family slowly, using chat rooms on the Internet.

I asked Kevin's Aunt Doris how the family could abandon him. I tried to see her point of view. She is eighty and lives in public housing for seniors. She is active in her church and sings in the choir. She worked as a stock clerk for CVS in a back-of-the-house job until she retired. She was married twice, but both her husbands died. She raised a daughter, who also died, and a niece and nephew whose parents were killed. She wrestles help from her niece and nephew, but they have problems too as their children struggle with adulthood. Her main support is her best friend Essie. They cook, shop, and travel together. Doris loves her relatives and works hard to keep in touch with them. She doesn't cast off people lightly. But Kevin's problems were too much for her. Like two other nephews before him, she decided that he was in God's hands. She will not help him anymore.

As families face the trauma of triaging kin, four political developments are making things harder for them.

Welfare reform was coming for a long time, as welfare mothers in particular were demonized under the Reagan and Clinton presidencies as lazy liabouts leaching off the state. Americans frustrated by their own low wages, overwork, and eroding family life seemed to respond to presidential rants on welfare. They thus supported a policy that will worsen their own work by glutting the labor market with more low-wage and needy workers. And it will cost more tax dollars than simple cash benefits. But as we have seen in earlier chapters, a hallmark of the credit and debt economy is that we look across a moral divide and see our credit others as pathological. Credit cards have worked like welfare and domestic partners in helping some middle-class people organize and time their lives, but rarely have they helped the poor. Women, especially black women, are termed unable to wait for grat-ification and the economic problems of both white and black women are couched in the language of dependency.

When welfare was reformed into Temporary Assistance for Needy Fam-ilies in 1996, mothers of children over one year old were required to work—even for nothing, and without adequate child care or transportation. If a woman could not find a job, she had to do community service in exchange for benefits. Tales of abuse abound, making the movement from welfare to work reminiscent of nineteenth-century poor relief. Sometimes women are assigned to private employers, who receive tax breaks for hiring them. They can work below minimum wage because their wages are defined as training wages for skills such as punctuality and hygiene. Sometimes they earn as lit-tle as $1 an hour, sometimes they wear specially designed and stigmatizing uniforms, and sometimes they are laid off and replaced with free convict labor.

Welfare reform eliminated the federal programs of the New Deal and the War on Poverty. Instead states received block grants, incentives to cut spending, and a good deal of latitude in paying benefits. Women could only receive benefits for a total of sixty months over their whole lives. Welfare benefits are often used to discipline women today. They can be docked if they refuse to identify the biological fathers of their children. They can be docked if their children miss school, pediatric appointments, or vaccina-tions. In some states, women who bear children while receiving benefits are denied future benefits because of a "family cap." Unemployment benefits have also been cut, and food stamps are much more difficult to get. In some places food stamps have been almost criminalized because recipients are fingerprinted. Nobody quite knows how poor women are supposed to leave abusive partners, supervise their children while holding multiple jobs, or cope with sickness, bills, and the complexities of making ends meet. And with all the talk about women's morals, the damage to the labor market was obscured as low-wage workers streamed in to compete for bad jobs. One morning I listened to two young mothers exchanging day care information at the busstop, and I imagined them swapping children—one would take care of the other's who was taking care of hers, both at inexpensive, low-wage, day care facilities. Overnight shifts in Washington are overpeopled with single mothers, and overnight child care centers thrive, upholding the long American tradition that every poverty program attracts predators—ra-pacious landlords, nursing home operators, land speculators, baby sitters for

the mentally challenged. But no matter what you do, you can't care for children free and work enough hours to earn a family wage.

Adding insult to injury, Citibank and Western Union contracted with
local governments to manage the ATM cards that would deliver welfare
benefits at $7.50 a pop. Some of the machines were free for recipients, but
they were disproportionately located in wealthy neighborhoods. Harlem,
with over fourteen thousand households receiving welfare payments, had
only six free machines. The machines failed frequently, and recipients found
it especially hard to access the cash back feature.[34] When a woman called
an 800 number to check on her funds, she most likely got a customer services representative in Bombay, where welfare jobs were outsourced to
young English speakers "trained in empathy." Outsourcing this kind of job
could send 3.3 million jobs overseas by 2015. Indian labor does research
and development, prepares tax returns, evaluates health insurance claims,
transcribes doctors' medical notes, analyzes financial data, duns for overdue
bills, reads CAT scans, creates presentations for investment banks, makes
reservations for Delta, provides bounced-check records to stores, and provides customer service to welfare and food-stamp recipients in nineteen
states. Credit card companies are especially enthusiastic about outsourcing,
although overseas workers have to learn to "pronounce both R's in Master-
Card." Lower labor costs in India allow them to chase smaller and smaller
outstanding payments, although one has to wonder what message welfare
to work program recipients are receiving.[35]

Another insulting outgrowth of welfare reform is the money now targeted for Individual Development Accounts, which aim to improve poor
people's attitudes toward saving, money management, and looking toward
the future. Social scientists are invited to apply to study and develop these
programs. The latest notice I received read like this:

Individual Development Accounts: The purpose of the program is to provide for
the establishment of demonstration projects designed to determine: the social, civic,
psychological, and economic effects of providing to individuals and families with
limited means an incentive to accumulate assets by saving a portion of their earned
income; the extent to which an asset-based policy that promotes saving for postsec-
ondary education, homeownership, and microenterprise development may be used
to enable individuals and families with limited means to increase their economic
self-sufficiency; and the extent to which an asset-based policy stabilizes and improves
families and the community in which the families live.

Susan Hyatt notes that these proposals are preposterous. They echo the
fantastic claims of anthropologist Oscar Lewis in 1959, who found among
the poor "a strong present-time orientation with relatively little disposition

to defer gratification," which Lewis thought to be a cause of poverty.[36] Hyatt argues that poor peoples' debt sustains a consumer economy for everybody. Financial institutions thus have no incentive whatsoever to help poor people save. They are the ones that need reform, not the lifeways of the poor.[37]

Similar views, however, shaped the Hope VI project, which cut through 165 public housing projects in the 1990s like a chainsaw in an abattoir. The goal of Hope VI was to demolish failed overbuilt developments from the 1960s and replace them with model, mixed-income projects. Middle-class people would live among the deserving poor, carefully screened for good credit and drug-fee histories, carefully disciplined so that they could not take in extra friends and relatives, and disciplined by constructive eviction if they misbehaved or failed to make payments. In many cities, only a few of the original residents could pass the credit test and wait for the new developments to be built. The new residents were often disproportionately old and living alone in small apartments never seriously intended for poor families. Nobody knew quite where the younger, bigger, more complex families went to live. They doubled up, tried to find private housing with Section 8 vouchers that landlords did not want to take and that did not go far in a tight housing market, became homeless, returned to the South, and in some cases simply squatted in their old buildings as they awaited demolition. Market rate renters and homeowners will enjoy most of the new housing. In Philadelphia only 36 of the 600 families displaced by Hope VI will ever be able to return. In other places the numbers run about one in five. In Chicago hundreds of squatters haunt the Ida B. Wells housing project, slated for demolition under Hope VI, and they will number among the homeless soon.[38]

Thus, Hope VI helped to make the poor disappear. They are more invisible now, their unsightly buildings blown up. Hope VI has undermined the ability of kinship and friendship networks to fight poverty by spreading them out, limiting their ability to take in kin, reinforcing triage, and squeezing the supply of affordable housing just as Temporary Assistance for Needy Families squeezed the supply of good-paying jobs. By 2002 minimum wage workers could not rent a two-bedroom unit in any U.S. city. Study after study has shown that landlords do not want Section 8 vouchers. Like welfare reformers, Hope VI advocates will not shut up about self-sufficiency. Their lectures must sound sour to poor people, who among many other problems, including—you guessed it—poor credit histories, manage terrible health situations, often without insurance. One in six poor adults reports a major depressive episode in the last twelve months—and where is the Prozac? Asthma in toxic cities is out of control. One in five poor children between the ages of six/fourteen has asthma, and for younger children the figures are one in four. However, some Hope VI programs offer credit counseling and budget management services, and people can always pawn their tools to buy over-the-counter inhalers.[39]

Hope VI also reinforced the problems in the food stamp program, which assumed that 30 percent of a family's budget would go for food. But now, when 80 percent of a family's budget must go for housing, food becomes expendable. Just as Robert Pollin noted in the 1980s, housing is the least flexible item in the family budget, and when housing costs are excessive, families go into debt for other necessities.

Hope VI was not reauthorized in September 2002, because President Bush and HUD Secretary Martinez seemed to have something even more hideous in mind. Modeled on Temporary Assistance for Needy Families, Housing Assistance for Needy Families will offer "new financing options and funding for buyer education." Good behavior in making twenty-four consecutive mortgage payments will be rewarded by reducing subsequent payments. In addition, the program will "make the mortgage process easier to understand." States will receive block grants to replace federal voucher programs so that they will have more flexibility. And Samaritan funds will be provided to help groups such as Habitat for Humanity.

The third problematic public policy is the War on Drugs: In the 1980s and 1990s the number of incarcerated Americans quadrupled. In 2002 America's prison population surged to 2.1 million, a 2.6 percent increase over 2001, the highest rate of incarceration of any country on earth. Mandatory sentences, especially for nonviolent drug offenders, are a major reason that inmate populations have risen for thirty years. Drug offenders now make up more than half of all federal prisoners. One out of every eight black men in their 20s and 30s are behind bars, compared with one in sixty-three whites. The large prison population cost the federal and state governments an estimated 40 billion dollars a year. When a prisoner is released, that individual is to become economically productive and resume the social responsibilities that are considered "normal" in this country, despite the fact that prisoners are stereotyped and maligned and receive virtually no help with rehabilitation or job training while in prison and may find it hard to clean up their credit histories there. The war on drugs has been an expensive failure, with its only tangible result punishing and warehousing people who might have been vital contributing members to their families and communities, but instead further strain them.[40]

Finally, there is the war on immigrants, who have long been personalized scapegoats for transnational political connections and recent structural adjustment programs. Immigrants cannot apply for financial aid to college without counting a sponsor's income as part of the total, and since welfare reform in 1996 they cannot apply for welfare or food stamps. These restrictions will not deter them from coming, but will certainly make life harder without the public safety net that once supplemented wages or offered a fair opportunity to receive a higher education. Immigrants often have their own supplemental predatory lending institutions. Many come with huge smuggling and transportation debts. For example, Peter Kwong writes that immigrants from Fuzhou and Wenzhou, in China, borrow $35,000–$40,000 to leave the depressed working conditions in urban, coastal factories. Their relatives are supposed to pay the loan off to the lenders, known affectionately as snakeheads, shortly after the new immigrant arrives. Then, over time, the immigrant repays his family, by working hard and saving. Ideally, he tries to save enough to help his relatives migrate as well. But with annual salaries at about $500 in China, relatives usually cannot pay the debt. So the immigrant assumes it at 30 percent interest. Usually they only earn enough to pay the interest portion of the loan, if that. This debt mangles kin ties. Immigrant parents cannot support their children and must send them back to China, or put them to work. Children leave school and sometimes join gangs. Debts turn relative against relative as snakeheads try to extort payments from transnational families. These immigrants work long hours in degraded conditions, often in hiding or in fear for their lives.[41]

In some places, fellow ethnics establish special credit facilities that help transfer money home. For example, where American Express charges as much as 24 percent of the amount wired, Salvadoran banks enter the market generally with lower fees. They are also eating into the former monopoly of Western Union and MoneyGram in the Salvadoran niche.[42] In some places coethnic lenders can act pretty loan-sharkish—lending at 104 to 260 percent a year to those the banks won't touch, taking collateral such as houses and gold chains and immigration papers.[43] In some Latino neighborhoods, these lenders are known as "prestamistas" and patronized although their interest rates are usurious and illegal (10 percent a week), because they are fast, reliable, and understanding, to a point. Immigrants also develop their own savings pool, like the Latino *tanda*, or the Korean *kye*. They contribute a certain amount weekly and then take turns borrowing from the pool.

KYLA'S STORY

Of the many stories that could be told, I will tell only one that illustrates the intersection of all four developments in the life of a young woman I will call Kyla. She came here as a child from Trinidad. She graduated from public high school and had a daughter when she was eighteen, who shows every sign of being as bright and charming as her mother is. They are inseparable. Kyla's mother has complicated personal problems, but she has recently found a man who is willing to support her. Kyla's youngest—and by all accounts brilliant—sister is in a halfway house for troubled adolescents. Her father died in Trinidad. Her younger brother is a lovable screwup who didn't finish high school but survives on his wits. He has always lived with Kyla. Kyla has never received any public assistance, but she has held a variety of interesting jobs, including visiting people who were injured in automobile accidents. A law firm paid her on commission for each one she could persuade to sue. Her baby's father, an excellent source of funds for support, was incarcerated a year ago for possession with intent to sell marijuana. At this point, Kyla returned to live with her great-hearted high-school boyfriend, who earns a steady living taking care of mentally challenged adults in his rented apartment. He took in her, her daughter, and her brother. He found Kyla part-time work, from 5 A.M. to 10 A.M. in a halfway house administered by the same company that employs him. She earns only enough there to support her somewhat lazy brother, who sometimes finds work through other Trinidadians who live in their apartment complex, but most often cannot work due to strict drug tests and his lack of a high school diploma. Although he has studied on his own for the GED for several years, he has not been able to pass it. One bright spot for Kyla is that the halfway house is down the street from her baby's godfather, one of two she enlisted as soon as she became pregnant. Although both are also poor, they help her with their time and child care.

Kyla steers clear of predatory lenders. However, in the summer of 2003, her brother received a secured card offer for a Platinum Visa card from First National Bank of Marin, located in Henderson, Nevada. I confiscated it to inspect the terms. Hawking no minimum income requirement, this card features an APR of 19.8 percent, a $99 application fee, a membership fee of $90 per year, to be paid mostly up front, a $29 late payment fee, $29 over the limit fee, multiple other little fees, and a security deposit of $200 for a credit line from $260 to $800 depending on credit history! He really wanted it, because he is desperate for cash. There is no other help in town for screwups who fail to graduate from the resource-starved public schools.

Thanks to cuts in social programs, Kyla's family has had no help: for her mother's addiction, her brother's unemployment, her underemployment, her sister's troubled brilliance, her daughter's education, food, and care. She simply has no safety net, but must overrely on men and part-time, badly paid work. There is almost no affordable housing, and she and her mother are totally dependent on the good will of men in their lives. I hope they will be able to hang on.

The year 2001 saw the biggest jump in American poverty in a decade. Nearly 12 percent of the population lived below the poverty line. In Washington, D.C., 109,500 residents live in poverty, or 20.2 percent of the population, and more than a quarter of African Americans live below the poverty line. In the neighborhoods decimated by Hope VI, ten have poverty rates above 30 percent, four over 40 percent, and in one, fully half the residents are poor.[44]

As families find they have less to give, emergency food outlets have blossomed in every city and town, like community supermarkets for hand me down food that has been damaged or lay on the shelf too long. Amtrak daily donates pita wraps that didn't sell. Liederman reports that one in three children in D.C. is malnourished. Stores too now have less to give, because once managers saw how much they were giving away, they began to rely more on scanning technologies and computerized inventories to plan more prudently.[45]

Government, too, apparently has less to give. A House resolution passed in 2003 requires Congressional committees to put forward legislation making $265 billion in cuts to entitlement programs over the next ten years. Of that amount, $165 billion will come from programs for the poor, such as Medicaid, nutrition assistance, school lunches, and food stamps.

Famous Pawn now occupies Will Harrison's flower shop, testifying to his inability to find affordable credit for his business. The same developers who refused to maintain or build low-cost urban housing have gone bust on overpriced condominiums, unnecessary office space, and underutilized shopping centers in the suburbs. The same lenders who disinvested in cities, jobs, workers, and infrastructure squandered their money on junk bonds, mergers, takeovers, and financial services. They are the ones who cannot defer gratification. Now they're back, extending credit to fringe banks for loans of last resort and thus passing on high-cost debt to the poor. They also take their cut of welfare. D.C. Mayor Anthony Williams offers businesses that will relocate to D.C. $8500 for each welfare to work recipient they hire.

The mythical media figures of wanton teen mothers and shoot-em-up drug dealers in an inner-city, science-fiction wasteland belie the fact that we are all participating in the same economy; we are all connected. Poor people are more scammed, redlined, and battered than isolated; and constructive investment in poor neighborhoods would be much more humane, productive, and helpful than endless speculation on the behavior of the poor or why poor women have their babies when they do.

When employment, government assistance, and intergenerational network flows fail them, when relatives can no longer provide small loans between checks, or exchange food stamps for cash, poor people develop strategies to work fringe banking. They pawn televisions and VCR's between checks, redeem them when they can, they cash their checks at America's Cash Express, pay their bills with money orders and moneygrams they purchase there, use the poor person's telephone, the pager, or a temporary cell phone, and sometimes "rent" grossly-overpriced furniture, cars, and appliances for as long as they can. And this debt poisons the credit careers that more and more define our autobiographies as citizens. When a person cannot get a job, a car, an apartment, a mortgage, or a bank account, and is thrust into the world of cash only, it is almost impossible to find your way out.

Chapter 6

Search for Solutions

Summer 2003: I bought something online from the Global Shopping Mall in New Delhi, India. It never came, the website shut down, and the telephone was disconnected. When I called to change my debit card the customer services rep began hawking overdraft protection, a checking plus credit line, and a Safety Check Savings Account over the phone. My much-loved family doctor was murdered by two nineteen-year-olds who were caught because they tried to use his credit cards online. Unlike me, they received their purchases, along with a visit from the police. At my doctor's sweltering funeral we used cardboard fans provided by AARP's Campaign Against Predatory Home Lending: "They didn't tell me I could lose my home. Get the facts before a bad loan gets you" wafted through the teary air. A few days later the feds announced that our credit records would be checked for security purposes every time we try to fly, and a lawyer from Rhode Island called to tell me I owed $700 to Capital One. I didn't even get a billing statement. The burden was on me to prove I did not owe the money. In July the *New York Times* ran a story about couples who plan lavish weddings right up to the limits on their assorted credit cards. Citigroup bought out the shaky Sears credit card portfolio to further swell their own. (For years, credit card operations had buttressed stand-alone retailers, but now Sears' credit card division had become a drag).[1] At the beachhouse where I fled for isolation to finish this book, Kelly of Debt Consolidation Services blared through the answering machine several times every day. This is really the way of the world.

War and occupation, harsh inequality, and assaults on our civil liberties are also the way of the world right now. New laws, elections, appointments, programs, policies, and verdicts are moving in the opposite direction of what I will suggest here. These events make it even more important not to lose hope or to fail to imagine a more just and equal world. Credit and debt are keys to injustice and inequality, and we must fight for far-reaching reforms in how they operate. The "orgy of exploitation" must stop.[2]

In this book, I have tracked the strategies of financial service companies to shirk productive investment for high-interest credit cards, student loans, and predatory lending. I have explored the fall of the middle class, the strangling of small business, the exploitation of college students, the battering of the poor, and the harsh inequalities refueled by the cost of credit to different social groups. The tentacles of debt have grown deep and hard. Debt drags us down, blocks our dreams, taints social relations, and casts great nets of spurious guilt and blame. If we do not blame ourselves, we pathologize our credit others. Taking on debt can make us feel grateful, generous, or independent at first, but it also thwarts empathy and fellow feeling.

We should not shower free credit on the wealthy, who too often use it foolishly and then expect the rest of us to bail them out. The mortgage interest tax deduction is almost a sacred entitlement, but we should at least cap it for the very wealthy. Renters should not face homelessness while millionaires deduct the interest on their mortgages. Another way to reduce debt inequality would be to charge convenience users a small fee for the free credit they enjoy each month. This way, people who revolve their balances and those such as college students and the poor who pay high interest, would not have to subsidize other people's no-cost loans. And the same, but more of it, goes for the tax deductions on the interest on junk bonds and leveraged buyouts. Investing in debt is not the most productive use of money.

When banks waste money on credit and debt, they rob us all, through slower economic growth, greater drags on families, and a raft of low-wage financial service jobs. The Federal Reserve Board, which encourages and discourages different uses of our money, is one of the most powerful institutions in the country. Its board of governors consists of seven members nominated by the President and confirmed by the Senate for fourteen-year terms. These governors meet with five district bank presidents in secret every five to eight weeks.[3] The board should be more open, democratic, and accountable, and less entangled with big banks. It should enact policies that support productive spending. For example, the Federal Reserve Board could deny deposit insurance to those banks that overindulge in highly leveraged mergers and acquisitions. Or it could raise the reserve requirements for banks that pile up their assets in credit card portfolios, encourage business flight overseas, or open subsidiaries to dabble in predatory lending. Control over the use of funds for borrowing is by no means unprecedented. There are margin requirements for investors who purchase stocks with borrowed funds. In the 1970s, Savings and Loan institutions were only permitted to lend money to buy homes. Regulations could be structured to require supporting the purchase of low-cost housing over, say, vacation homes.

These policies could be reinforced by the tax code. For example, a small sales tax on all financial transactions would raise the cost of wanton speculation. The tax advantages enjoyed by pension funds could be tied to socially responsible lending and more of a voice for labor unions in how funds are invested. In addition, government could encourage productive investment by taxing short-term gains, giving credit for long-term holdings, and developing rules that encourage investments that create living wage jobs.

The rich must pay their share of taxes on both income and wealth. We should return to the tax rates of the 1970s. The inequality of our country is too harsh, the rich simply too rich. And too much of their wealth comes from interest on the debt of others: our mortgages, the interest we pay the pawnshop, the interest poor countries pay through structural adjustment, and the soaring deficits of the imperial American government.[4]

In Chapter 3, I wrote of the failed campaign for usury caps on lending. Federal law should enforce usury caps on all types of lending and tame the out-of-control fees through which lenders make many of their profits. I almost admire banks' seemingly endless energy and creativity in inventing and reinventing fees. Today it appears that they are riding high on the penalties for bounced checks, which have become high-interest, regulation-evading loans with limits of $100 to $300 at an annual percentage rate of 1000 percent or more. Even payday loans are less expensive.[5] But enough is enough Government should pressure credit card companies to forgive householders' debts, or at least ease the terms of repayment and the mushrooming interest that accrues too relentlessly and fast. We should also pressure international lending agencies to forgive Third World debt, or at least soften the harsh conditions through which other countries pay back their loans.

Higher education has become an unfunny joke in this country, saddling students with intractable debt and the prospect of boiler room jobs in the financial services industry. We should ban credit card solicitors from college campuses, or demonstrate against them when they are there, but that is only a first step. We can look back with pride on the success of the GI Bill in boosting white working-class men into the middle class, and we can build on that lesson to extend affordable higher education to the rest of America. We could simply chip away at the problem. We could declare an amnesty on student loans entirely. Or we could at least ask that the federal government fully institute direct lending, so that large bureaucracies and banks cannot bilk student loans for high salaries and profits. We could make national service a reasonable alternative to repaying student loans. We could make sure that low-income students receive grants. But the best course of action would be to make higher education free. More access to higher education will mean more participation in the political system. Higher enrollments will fuel the expansion of college and universities, which could stimulate jobs in areas ranging from construction to teaching. The government could provide an education to everyone currently in school for a tiny percent of the federal budget. We should think hard about making a college education more like the entitlement that it is for citizens in many European countries.[6]

We also need programs that tighten and enrich the job market that students face after they graduate. Every year I see more college graduates working in restaurants, grocery stores, and health clubs, peddling financial advice or mortgages, dunning errant debtors and collecting bills as low-paid telemarketers, and feeling slightly more fortunate than those high school graduates staffing check-cashing outlets and pawn shops or working as repo men at minimum wage. Tripling the salary paid teachers would be a good start. Or we could look to the model of the New Deal, which hired youth for conservation programs, unemployed men for public works, and writers and artists for creative, living-wage jobs. We would ensure that women could participate in these programs too, as did the Comprehensive Education and Training Act in the 1970s. These jobs offered people skills-building, living-wage jobs to work in and help shore up community-based organizations such as women's health clinics. Public works jobs could also be dedicated to the conversion of military equipment and waste, high performance organic farming, solar energy conversion, affordable housing, state of the art schools, health-care facilities, and mass transit.[7]

The Living Wage movement has campaigned for wages that can sustain a reasonable quality of life. Promoting full employment at decent wages, so workers can afford to spend money, would also promote overall spending in the economy. This policy could lead to inflation, as it did in the 1970s, because workers will have the power to bid up their wages and businesses will respond by raising prices. Inflation could hurt retired people on fixed incomes and the lowest paid workers, as well as whose major source of income is interest. But inflation can be tempered if workers receive non-wage benefits, and if basic social protections moderate wage demands.[8] We should also strengthen workers' rights to organize unions.

The rise of predatory lending to meet everyday and emergency needs of poor people testifies to the lack of constructive investment and affordable lending in poor communities, to say nothing of the absolute dearth of living-wage jobs, affordable housing, and social safety nets there. Banks have abandoned and then ravaged central cities, as the failure of the Community Reinvestment Act, which mandated responsible lending there. The conservative bureaucracies of the four federal agencies charged with administering the Community Reinvestment Act have never really supported it. Early challenges to the Community Reinvestment Act were repeatedly denied by the Federal Reserve Board, which has stuck to a narrow interpretation of the act. The board has ruled repeatedly that the purpose of the act is to ensure comprehensive marketing and communication between banks and communities about what kinds of credit banks offer. Then the bank must offer everybody in the community equal access to that credit. The board has declined to intervene in what it calls the "product mix" of a bank — its array of mortgages, credit cards, and small business loans, for example.[9] Banks and the Federal Reserve Board have subverted the intent of the Community Reinvestment Act and the reasonable goals of activists who have used the act to challenge bankers' lending practices. Even when the act has been reformed and strengthened, for example in 1994–1996, it has relied heavily on on-the-ground evaluators who have too much latitude in resolving disputes. Some wonderful programs have come from the Community Reinvestment Act, but sometimes these have created small islands of investment that are not linked to the needs of the neighborhood around them. The Community Reinvestment Act has not lived up to its promise.

We should strengthen and enforce the Community Reinvestment Act and the other acts that aimed to protect us from predators, such as the Home Mortgage Disclosure Act and the Home Ownership and Equity Protection Act. We should extend the Community Reinvestment Act to cover fringe banks, insurance companies, mortgage companies, and other quasi-banks operating in our communities. We should insist that banks guarantee low-cost banking services to the poor. We should abolish, not just thoroughly regulate, predatory lending. Cities and states are battling out these regulations in several places, and the industry appears to be looking toward the federal government to override local restrictions on their practices. But activists including Acorn, the AARP, and the NAACP have done well at pressuring local governments to cap the predators' usorious rates or at least to link them to other interest rates.

Banks should also serve the credit needs of inner city neighborhoods more imaginatively. This means more than simply responding fairly to loan applications. It means working collaboratively with residents to determine their needs and offering appropriate, affordable, and productive credit that will not burden them excessively. We need much more affordable housing, in dense, diversified neighborhoods with shops, social services fired-up schools, parks, and jobs. The Community Reinvestment Act should ensure that small business owners have access to affordable credit, and that bankers and government fund public works jobs

Banks that are too big should also be smaller, geographically narrower, and more accountable to their communities.[10] Smaller, more local banks would defy the radically new, giant banks enabled by recent hallmark laws: the Interstate Banking and Branching Act of 1994 and the Financial Services Modernization Act of 1999. The first law allowed banks to expand across state lines without the bother of setting up anything new, like a board of directors. The bank could simply open a branch of itself. This interstate branching has allowed massive evasions of the Community Reinvestment Act, because each big bank has too many parts to investigate, each branch is too small a part of a huge whole to seem to matter. It is all bulked up for global financial combat rather than tuned in to the needs of an irksome local community. The Financial Services Modernization Act enabled banks to join forces with brokerage houses and insurance companies. It removed the 1930s firewall between these kinds of institutions, which was designed to prevent risky in-house speculation, lending, and possible depression. We are dealing here with monstrous hybrids. It's no wonder the Community Reinvestment Act can't touch them.

Despite their daunting sound, we should pay attention to these laws, and repeal them. Otherwise, we will continue to see bigger and bigger banks. For example, in early 2004 J.P. Morgan merged with Bank One to produce a single behemoth with a wide mix of retail outlets, corporate clients, clients for deposits, mortgages, and credit cards.[11] Because today's economy is so debt-ridden and so fragile, we face the unholy specter of bailing out these institutions that rampage so wildly and do so much harm.

All over the world, we need to ensure that families have a safety net of public support and that that they are not punished and incarcerated via victimless crimes. Jeff Maskovsky writes powerfully of what he calls the "workist consensus" that drives policies such as welfare reform, which loosens the labor market and further polarizes income by forcing poor people, even mothers of young children providing crucial domestic service and day care into low-wage jobs. We should restore payments to parents at home rather than driving them into working poverty and debt. We can abandon individualized, distorted, privatist myths of individual responsibility and reaffirm our social responsibility to tighten the labor market, make wages and incomes more equal, and provide a safety net for people who are vulnerable.[12] We should expand federal, state, and local government support for education, childcare, health, environmental protection, and public infrastructure investments—to stimulate overall spending in the short run and promote higher productivity and general well-being in the long run.

For years, we have heard that consumers must keep shopping in order for the economy to prosper. The national consumer is the giddy housewife writ large, a mystification. The stock market bubble of the 1990s was out of touch with the rest of the economy, which citizens had to be willing to sustain by taking on debt. But debt-financed personal consumption is not a good way to subsidize, indirectly, the social good.

Consumer capitalism has gone mad. Corporations seeking profit for themselves rampage wildly throughout the world in search of cheap labor and high profits. Governments and international lending agencies help them suppress labor costs and increase social costs through tax breaks, environmental deregulation and the battering of labor. People in many places work too hard for low wages and mounting debt. Businesses produce too much stuff and waste and excess that we are increasingly unable to buy. We take on huge debt to import things and then inflict that model in other places through structural adjustment, so nobody can produce their own food or medicines anymore. Once people stop borrowing to buy, it's all over. Governments must liquidate debt burdens and invest in doing things differently, beginning with more regulations on globe-trotting businesses such as levying taxes on their transactions. This harsh inequality, overproduction, and long-distance, debt-financed consumption of badly distributed goods and services is not really good for anybody. Labor is too beaten down, and erstwhile consumers all tapped out. As I have argued throughout this book, debt is the engine that drives all this, the bloodsucker that makes us anxious and mean-spirited and drags us down. We tend to call it credit, which emphasizes its good parts. Credit can help us through emergencies and give us a fresh start. But credit becomes debt when it is so laden with interest and fees that it is impossible to pay back. The social relations are oppressive, not liberating, the fresh start is always elusive.[13]

Notes

Chapter 1

1. Gordon Dutter, "Write against H.R. 10," *Metro Justice* 1–2, http://www.metrojustice.org/news98/May98; Karen L. Grandstrand, "Congress Repealed Glass-Steagall, But Regulators Are Drafting a Replacement, Frederikson & Byron, P.A. 1–3," http://www.fredlaw.com/articles/banking/bank, July 10, 2003; William Greider, "Crime in the Suites," *The Nation*, February 4, 2002, 11–14; Julie Houston, "The Glass-Steagall Menagerie," http://www.bankrate.com/brm.news.advice, July 1, 2003; Gretchen Morgenson, "Caution: This Hybrid Can Sting," *New York Times*, March 9, 2003, 1, 10.
2. William Greider, "Deflation," *The Nation*, June 30, 2003, 12.
3. Abby Scher, "Credit Card Pushers Pump Up Profits—and Risk," *Dollars and Sense* (November/December 1998): 21.
4. Robert Scheer, "Another Bankrupt Idea from Congress," *Los Angeles Times*, July 30, 2002.

Chapter 2

1. Lendol Calder, *Financing the American Dream: A Cultural History of Consumer Credit* (Princeton, N.J.: Princeton University Press, 1999).
2. Warren Belasco, *Americans on the Road* (Cambridge, Mass.: MIT Press, 1979).
3. Calder, *Financing the American Dream*.
4. Neil McMillen, *Dark Journey* (Urbana: University of Illinois Press, 1989).
5. Joseph Nocera, *A Piece of the Action* (New York: Simon and Schuster, 1994), 54.
6. See Lewis Mandel, *The Credit Card Industry* (Boston: Twayne, 1990); Nocera, *Piece of the Action*; and George Ritzer, *Expressing America* (Thousand Oaks: Pine Forge Press, 1995) for overviews of the development of the credit card industry.
7. Nocera, *Piece of the Action*, 68–69.
8. Thomas Durkin, "Credit Card Holding and Use Among American Families: Results of National Surveys [1977 and 1978]," *Journal of Retail Banking* 2 (June 1980): 19–26; Joel P. Friedman, "The Changing World of Plastic Cards: A Revolution in Perspective," *Journal of Retail Banking* 9, no. 1 (spring 1987): 7–16; Elizabeth Hirschman, Mark I. Alpert, and Rajendra K. Strivastava, "Consumer Credit Card Usage and Retail Purchasing," *Journal of Retail Banking* 2, no. 1 (March 1980): 54–65.
9. Robert Manning, *Credit Card Nation* (New York: Basic Books, 2000).
10. David Nye, "The Energy Crisis of the 1970s as a Cultural Crisis," *European*

Contributions to American Studies [Netherlands] 1997: 82–102; David Ranney, *Global Decisions, Local Collisions* (Philadelphia: Temple University Press, 2003).

11. American dollars were so widespread because of an agreement made at Bretton Woods after World War II that the United States was the most powerful and stable country at the end of the war. The U.S. dollar anchored other currencies from then until 1971. So many oil dollars were deposited in American banks that Senator Frank Church instigated an investigation of them in 1974. See Ranney, *Global Decisions*.

12. Ellen Frank, "Focus on the Fed," *Dollars and Sense* 202 (November/December 1995): 8, 9, 38, 39.

13. Nancy MacLean, "Liberalism Implodes: What Happened When White Women Brought Affirmative Action to Hiring in Higher Education" (workshop paper presented at Northwestern University, Evanston, February 4, 2003).

14. See Joyce Gelb and Marian Lief Palley, "Women and Interest Group Politics," *American Politics Quarterly* 3, no. 3 (July 1987): 331–62. Betty Furness is quoted on p. 336. See also Gary Chandler and John Coffman, "A Comparative Analysis of Empirical vs. Judgmental Credit Evaluation," *Journal of Retail Banking* 1, no. 2 (1979): 15–26; John L. Culhane, "The Eye of the Beholder: Developments under the Equal Credit Opportunity Act and Regulation B," *Business Lawyer* 46, no. 3 (May 1991): 1069–76; Dolores Smith, "Revision of the Board's Equal Credit Regulation: An Overview," *Federal Reserve Bulletin* (December 1985): 913–20. Later Senator Carl Levin and then Representative Joe Kennedy introduced legislation banning discrimination by zip code, but neither was successful. See, for example, Peter Lucas, "Cards for All: No Matter Where They Live," *Credit Card Management* 4, no. 3 (June 1991): 600–666.

15. Michael Quint, "Banks Raise Scrutiny of Credit Cards," *New York Times*, May 27, 1991, 1, 36; Daniel Mendel-Black and Evelyn Richards, "Peering into Private Lives," *Washington Post*, January 20, 1991, H1, H4, H6.

16. Patricia Roos and Barbara Reskin, "Occupational Desegregation in the 1970s: Integration and Economic Equity," *Sociological Perspectives* 35, no. 1 (1992): 69–91; Dorothy Sue Cobble, " 'A Spontaneous Loss of Enthusiasm': Workplace Feminism and the Transformation of Women's Service Jobs in the 1970s," *International Labor and Working-Class History* 56 (1999): 23–44; Nancy MacLean, "The Hidden History of Affirmative Action: Working Women's Struggles in the 1970s and the Gender of Class," *Feminist Studies* 25, no. 1 (1999): 42–78; Marisa Chappell, "Rethinking Women's Politics in the 1970s," *Journal of Women's History* 13, no. 4 (2002): 155–79.

17. MacLean, "Liberalism Implodes."

18. Patrick J. Akard, "Corporate Mobilization and Political Power: The Transformation of U.S. Economic Policy in the 1970s," *American Sociological Review* 57 (1992): 597–615; The Editors, "Creeping Stagnation," *Monthly Review* 38, no. 8 (January 1977): 1–14.

19. David Segal, "The All-Volunteer Force in the 1970s," *Social Science Quarterly* 79, no. 2 (1998): 390–411.

20. Calder, *Financing the American Dream*.

21. W. Dunkelberg, "Economic and Distributive Effects of Credit Regulation," Credit Research Center Reports, Purdue University, 1977.

22. Ralph Rohne, "Marquette: Bad Law and Worse Policy," *Journal of Retail Banking* 1, no. 1 (1978): 76–84; "Marquette: A Sound Legislative and Social Result," *Journal of Retail Banking* 1, no. 1 (1978): 85–96.

23. I thank Scott Bewley for alerting me to this institution. See also Andrew Taylor, "Interstate Banking Law: For the Record," *Congressional Quarterly*, December 3, 1994, 3461–63.

24. Ward Churchill, "The Bloody Wake of Alcatraz: Political Repression of the American Indian Movement During the 1970s," *American Indian Culture and Research Journal* 18, no. 4 (1994): 253–300; Julian Zelizer, "Bridging State and Society," *Social Science History* 24, no. 2 (summer 2000): 379–93.

25. Frank Levy, "The Vanishing Middle Class and Related Issues: A Review of Living Standards in the 1970s and 1980s," *PS: Political Science and Politics* 20, no. 3 (1987): 650–55. Evidence for the well-organized agenda of business in the 1970s lies in its successful resistance to the Consumer Protection Agency and the labor law reforms that Congress wanted to pass, as well as in the Bankruptcy Reform Act that business PACs initiated, which allowed for much cheaper and faster corporate bankruptcies.

26. William E. Leuchtenberg, *In the Shadow of FDR* (Ithaca, N.Y.: Cornell University Press, 1993), 184, 186.

27. Gary M. Fink and Hugh Davis Graham, *The Carter Presidency* (Lawrence: University Press of Kansas, 1998).

28. Thomas Borstelmann, *The Cold War and the Color Line* (Cambridge, Mass.: Harvard University Press, 2001); Ken Kusmer, "Culture and Politics in a Conservative Age," published in Italian as "L'America in Crisi," *Leggendaria: Libri, Letture, Linguaggi* 39 (summer 2003): 8–13; Leuchtenberg, *In the Shadow of FDR*, 178.

29. Stanley E. Morris, "Consumer Credit Controls: Risks and Lessons." *Journal of Retail Banking* 11, no. 2 (June 1980): 1–10; Robert Samuelson, "Don't Throw Away Your Cards Yet—Plastic Economy Is Far from Dead," *National Journal*, June 7, 1980, 924–28; Charlotte H. Scott, "Protecting the Consumer after Credit Restraint," *Journal of Retail Banking* 11, no. 4 (December 1980): 27–35.

30. Liz Roman Gallese, "Going Slow: Banks Ease Up Pushing Credit Cards as High Cost of Money Eats into Profits," *Wall Street Journal*, January 3, 1980, 32; *U.S. News and World Report*, March 31, 1980, 29–30; John T. Wooley, "Exorcising Inflation-Mindedness: The Transformation of Economic Management in the 1970s," *Journal of Policy History* 10, no. 1 (1998): 130–52.

31. See Rene Ramirez, "Simplified Consumer Credit Forms: Plain English Compliance Standards," *Journal of Retail Banking* 1, no. 3 (December 1979): 36–45. See also Lynn C. Goldfaden and Gerald P. Hurst, "Regulatory Responses to Changes in the Consumer Financial Services Industry," *Federal Reserve Bulletin* (February 1985): 75–81; Paul H. Schieber and Dennis Replansky, *Consumer Compliance and Anti-Discrimination Laws* (Chicago: Probus Publishing Company, 1991).

32. "Data for Sale," *Consumer Reports* (January 1996): 34. See also Peter H. Lewis, "Forget Big Brother," *New York Times*, March 19, 1998, E1, E6; Caroline E. Mayer, "Measure Would Hold Credit Reports Up to the Light," *Washington Post*, November 7, 2003, E1, E10.

33. Matt Richtel, "Credit Card Theft Is Thriving Online as Global Market," *New York Times*, May 13, 2002, A1, A14.

34. Gregory Bozcar, "What to Expect When the Bank Examiners Come—and Turn Their Attention to Your CRA Record," *ABA Banking Journal* (April 1979): 35–42; "C RA Reform Put to the Test," *Secondary Mortgage Markets (A Freddie Mac Quarterly)* 13, no. 1 (February 1996): 3–6; Janice Perlman, "Grassrooting the System," *Social Policy* (September/October 1976): 4–20; Gregory D. Squires, ed., *From Redlining to Reinvestment* (Philadelphia: Temple University Press, 1992).

35. Edmund Danziger, "A New Beginning or the Last Hurrah: American Indian Response to Reform Legislation of the 1970s," *American Indian Culture and Research Journal* 7, no. 4 (1983): 69–84.

36. Tom Robbins, "Hard Times at the Co-op Bank," *City Limits* (January/June 1982): 20–22.

37. See Stephanie Coontz, *The Way We Never Were* (New York: Basic Books, 1992); Kenneth Jackson, *Crabgrass Frontier* (New York: Oxford University Press, 1985); Karen Brodkin, *How Jews Became White Folks and What That Says About Race in America* (New Brunswick, N.J.: Rutgers University Press, 1999).

38. Penelope Mitchell, "What Do Board Games Teach Us? A Look at Monopoly and Mall Madness," *The Graduate Review* (1996): 92–97.

39. Elizabeth Hirschman, Mark I. Alpert, and Rajendra K. Srivastava, "Customer Credit Card Usage and Retail Purchasing," *Journal of Retail Banking* 11, no. 1 (March 1980): 54–65; Richard L. Peterson, "Occupation, Employment and Consumer Loan Defaults," *Journal of Retail Banking* 11, no. 2 (June 1980): 28–38.

40. Elizabeth Kaplan, "A Hot New Strategy for Credit Cards," *Dun's Business Monthly* 127, no. 2 (February 1986): 46–47.

41. Terry Lefton, "Co-branding Reshapes Credit Landscape," *Adweek*, October 4, 1993, 16.

42. Edmond Sanders, "Tricky Business," *Chicago Tribune* (North Suburban Classified/Section 6), August 16, 1997, 1, 13.

43. Albert Crenshaw, "On Balance, a Credit Card Squeeze," *Washington Post*, October 10, 1997, G1, G2.

44. Helene Duffy, "Marketing for Survival: Credit Card Strategies for the '90s," *Superbrands*, October 18, 1993, 79–81. For a slightly different perspective, see "Card Perks: Worthwhile and Worthless," *Consumer Reports* (January 1996): 33.

45. Albert Crenshaw, "Taking Credit for a Card-Using Boom," *Washington Post*, October 17, 1993, H1, H3; "Picking What's in the Cards for You," *Washington Post*, February 27, 1994, H1, H3; Albert Crenshaw and Jerry Knight, "Playing Their Cards Just Right?" *Washington Post*, May 31, 1995, A1, A6; Melissa Della Posta, "Use Your MasterCard, Plant a Tree," *Catalog Age* 8, no. 8 (August 1991): 16–17; Allison Fahey, "MasterCard Scores," *Advertising Age*, March 25, 1991, 3, 45; "Visa Heads Olympic Ads," *Advertising Age*, July 8, 1991, 3; Sanders, "Tricky Business"; Anthony Faiola and Albert B. Crenshaw, "Marketing by the Miles," *Washington Post*, April 21, 1996, H1, H5; Linda Punch, "A Household Name," *Credit Card Management* 6, no. 5 (August 1993): 30–31.

46. Dina ElBoghdady, "Banks, Retailers Again Push 'Co-Branded' Credit Cards," *Washington Post*, October 14, 2003, E1, E5.

Chapter 3

1. Donald Barlett and James Steele, *America: What Went Wrong?* (Kansas City: Andrews and McMeel, Inc. 1992).

2. Paul Allen, "And Next for Retail Credit . . . Boom or Bust for Bankers?" *Journal of Retail Banking* 9, no. 4 (winter 1987–88): 5–15. See also Robert Avery, Gregory Elliehausen, and Arthur B. Kennickell, "Changes in Consumer Installment Debt: Evidence from the 1983 and 1986 Surveys of Consumer Finances," *Federal Reserve Bulletin* 73, no. 10 (October 1987): 761–68; Glenn Canner, "Changes in Consumer Holding and Use of Credit Cards: 1970–86," *Journal of Retail Banking* 10, no. 1

(spring 1988): 13–24; "Use Patterns Among U.S. Families," *Journal of Retail Banking* 7, no. 3 (fall 1985): 63–74 ; Michael Lenora, "Segmenting Credit Cardholders by Behavior," *Journal of Retail Banking* 13, no. 1 (spring 1991): 19–23.

3. Glenn Canner and Anthony Cyrnak, "Recent Developments in Credit Card Holding and Use Patterns Among U.S. Families," *Journal of Retail Banking* 8, no. 3 (fall 1985): 63–74.

4. Canner and Cyrnak, "Recent Developments."

5. Glenn Canner and Anthony Cyrnak, "Determinants of Consumer Credit Card Usage Patterns," *Journal of Retail Banking* 8, nos. 1 and 2 (spring/summer 1986): 9–18. See also Linda Punch, "The Latest Anti-Attrition Tool: More Credit," *Credit Card Management* 5, no. 5 (August 1992): 48–51.

6. Allen, "And Next for Retail Credit."

7. Allen, "And Next for Retail Credit," 8–9.

8. Theresa Sullivan, Elizabeth Warren, and Jay Lawrence Westbrook, *As We Forgive Our Debtors* (New York: Oxford University Press, 1989). See also Peter Lucas, "Thumbs up for the Tube's Card Ads," *Credit Card Management* 5, no. 8 (November 1992): 12–16.

9. Stephen Brosch, "Consumer Attitudes Toward Credit Cards," *Credit World* 80, no. 5 (July/August 1992): 8–13.

10. Roger Blackwell and Margaret Hanke, "The Credit Card and the Aging Baby Boomer," *Journal of Retail Banking* 9, no. 1 (spring 1987): 17–24. Quotes are from pp. 17, 18.

11. Blackwell and Hanke, "The Credit Card and the Aging Baby Boomer," 24.

12. Katy Butler, "The Great Boomer Bust," *Mother Jones* (June 1989): 33–38. Quote is on p. 36. See also Robert Pollin, *Deeper in Debt: The Changing Financial Conditions of U.S. Households* (Washington, D.C.: Economic Policy Institute, 1990), 17–18.

13. Pollin, *Deeper in Debt*. See also Frank Levy, *Dollars and Dreams* (New York: W. W. Norton 1987).

14. Sandra Crockett, "Till Debt Do Us Part," *Baltimore Sun*, July 29, 1996, D1, D2.

15. Andrew Tobias, "Take Control of Your Credit Cards," *Parade*, November 1, 1998, 4, 5.

16. Albert Crenshaw, "Where Consumer Credit Is Due," *Washington Post*, October 21, 1990, A1, A21, A22; "Tips for Yule Shoppers: Don't Leave Home with It," *Washington Post*, October 23, 1994, H1, H4; Kenneth Eskey, "Pay Cash for Christmas," *Killeen Daily Herald*, December 4, 1989; Harville Hendrix, "Holiday Stress," *Family Circle*, December 19, 1989, 192–98; Craig Mellon, "By Debt Possessed," *Across the Board* (January 1985): 5–8; Andrea Rock, "Holiday Budget Busters and How to Avoid Them," *Family Circle*, December 19, 1989, 19–21; Editorial, "Don't Overspend During the Holidays," *Sunbeam* (Salem, N.J.), December 15, 1989.

17. Susan Jacoby, "Money Trouble," *Glamour* (April 1992): 266, 267, 297.

18. "Fewer Cardholders Revolve Balances," *Credit Union Magazine* 58, no. 6 (June 1992): 15–17; Jon Nordheimer, "Young, Successful but Between Jobs," *New York Times*, November 7, 1990, 1; Pollin, *Deeper in Debt*, 12–15; Linda Punch, "A Sobering Year for Collectors," *Credit Card Management* 5, no. 3 (June 1992): 52–56; Stanley Slom, "Credit Use Drops: Customers Write More Checks as They Try to Control Debt," *Stores* 73, no. 9 (September 1991): 46, 51; John Stewart, "The New Frugality," *Credit Card Management* 5, no. 2 (May 1992): 28–29.

19. Teresa Wiltz, "Fantastic Plastic Can Leave You Feeling Spent," *Chicago Tribune*, August 16, 1998.

20. Rex Wolfe, "Get Out of Debt Overnight No Matter How Much You Owe," *Weekly World News*, October 1, 1996, 8, 9, 41.

21. Hank Steuvern, "Just One Word: Plastic. Why We Owe Our Souls to Wilmington, Delaware," *Washington Post Magazine*, June 14, 2002, 20, 26.

22. Ray Schultz, "Hungry Marketers Chew on the Credit Starved," *Business and Society Review* 78 (summer 1991): 33–38.

23. Louis Uchitelle, "The Rise of the Losing Class," *New York Times*, November 20, 1994, 2, 5; Brett Williams, "Babies and Banks: The 'Reproductive Underclass' and the Raced, Gendered Masking of Debt," in *Race*, ed. Steven Gregory and Roger Sanjek (New Brunswick, N.J: Rutgers University Press, 1995); Michael Wines, "The Indignant Middle Class Is Also on the Dole," *New York Times*, section 4, November 20, 1994, 5.

24. Tom Ryan, "Lighten Up," *US Air: The EntertainAir* (December 1994); Charlene Sullivan and Debra Worden, "Bankruptcy in a Bank Credit Card Portfolio," *Journal of Retail Banking* 13, no. 4 (Winter 1991–92): 33–40.

25. Ryan, "Lighten Up."

26. Katherine Morrall, "Dear Deadbeat: Collections and Recovery," *Credit Card Management* 5, no. 8 (November 1992): 18–21.

27. Kaplan, "A Hot New Strategy," 47.

28. Jennifer Bayout, "For Richer or Poorer, to Our Visa Card Limit," *New York Times*, July 13, 2003, 1, 17; Jon Berry, "Shuffling the Cards," *Adweek's Marketing Week*, October 7, 1991, 4; Robert Burns, "Finding Bankruptcy's Villains," *Credit Union Magazine* 5, no. 3 (1991): 35, 37; "Survey of Retail Credit Trends: Supermarkets," *Chain Store Age Executive* 68, no. 1 (January 1992): 32B–33B; "Pier 1 Imports Company Cards That Work," *Chain Store Age Executive* 68, no. 2 (February 1992): 77–78; Albert Crenshaw, "Credit Card Firms Compete to Keep Users Charged Up," *Washington Post*, May 14, 1995, H1, H6; Scott Donaton and Gary Levin, "AmEx Heads Downscale," *Advertising Age*, October 12, 1992, 1, 47; Carrie Goerne, "Buying Groceries on Credit: Growing Numbers of Shoppers Prefer to Pay with Plastic," *Marketing News*, September 28, 1992,1, 11; Patricia Kuhn, "Charge It: Credit and Debit Cards Come to the Public Sector," *Government Finance Review* 8, no. 3 (June 1992): 13–16; Linda Punch, "Credit Cards and the Health Care Crisis, *Credit Card Management* 5, no. 4 (July 1992): 28–40; Gary Shilling, "Plastic Bombs," *Forbes*, July 22, 1991; "And on the Seventh Day, Everyone Shopped," *Washington Post*, June 12, 1995, 3; Albert Crenshaw, "Holders of Credit Cards Can Cut Deals or Get Out," *Washington Post*, February 24, 1991, H3, 24; Jayne Pearl, "Finding the Best Credit Card," *Working Woman* (April 1993): 28, 29, 104; Michael Quint, "Favored Credit Card Holders Quietly Receive Lower Rates," *New York Times*, November 13, 1991, A1, C8; Slom, "Credit Use Drops"; Michael Sullivan, "Bank Marketing Strategy: Reshuffling the Cards," *Bankers Monthly* 109, no. 11 (November 1992): 27.

29. "House of Cards," *Consumer Reports* (January 1996): 31, 32; Albert Crenshaw, "Jumps in Credit Card Rates Bring Congressional Scrutiny," *New York Times*, May 29, 2003, A1, C4; Nicholas Johnston, "Capital One Financial Chief Quits," *Washington Post*, March 4, 2003, E1; Jennifer Bayout, "Capital One Officer, Facing U.S. Inquiry, Quits," *New York Times*, March 4, 2003, C1, C9; Scher, "Credit Card Pushers."

30. David Morrow, "The Hit Quiz Show for Those Who Owe," *New York Times*, August 11, 1996, 1, 8; David Zurawik, "Tuning in to Hard Times," *Baltimore Sun*, June 23, 1996, J1, J7.

31. David Warsh, "Credit Card Cap Is One Way to Treat an Addiction," *Washington Post*, November 27, 1991, C3.

32. Tobias, "Take Control of Your Credit Cards."

33. Margaret Talbot, "Debt Voyeurs," *New York Times Magazine*, July 18, 1999, 11, 12.

34. Jeanne Wright, "Binge, Splurge: Shoppers Bag Ingenuity on the Road to Mastering Deceit's Possibilities," *Chicago Tribune*, January 24, 1993.

35. Vince Passaro, "Who'll Stop the Drain? Reflections on the Art of Going Broke," *Harper's Magazine* August 1998, 35–42. Quote is on p. 36.

36. Katherine Newman, *Declining Fortunes* (New York: Basic Books, 1993).

37. Barbara Ehrenreich, *Fear of Falling* (New York: Panheon Books, 1989).

38. Tobias, "Take Control," 5.

39. Passaro, "Who'll Stop the Drain?" 36.

40. Barbara Gilder Quint, "How I Got Out of Credit-Card Debt," *Glamour* (May 1995): 133–36.

41. Jane Bryant Quinn, "Money Facts," *Woman's Day*, November 3, 1992: 22.

42. I thank Maureen Fleming, Tom Grooms, Regina Harrison, Susan Lanser, Joan Radner, and Rodger Streitmatter for these insights.

43. Passaro, "Who'll Stop the Drain?" 40.

44. William Roseberry, "Marxism and Culture," in *The Politics of Culture*, ed. Brett Williams (Washington, D.C.: Smithsonian Press, 1991).

45. Charlene Sullivan, "Consumer Credit: Are There Limits?" *Journal of Retail Banking* 8, no. 4 (winter 1986/87): 5–13.

46. Martha Seger, "Statement Before the Subcommittee on Consumer Affairs and Coinage of the Committee on Banking, Housing, and Urban Affairs," U.S. Senate, April 21, 1987, *Federal Reserve Bulletin* (June 1987): 430–37.

47. Crenshaw and Knight, "Playing Their Cards" (emphasis added).

48. Glenn Canner and James Fergus, "The Economic Effects of Proposed Ceilings on Credit Card Interest Rates," *Federal Reserve Bulletin* (January 1987): 1–13; "The Effects on Consumers and Creditors of Proposed Ceilings on Credit Card Interest Rates," *Board of Governors of the Federal Reserve System* (October 1987): 1–26; Charlotte H. Scott, "The Fairness Issue in Credit Card Pricing," *Journal of Retail Banking* 8, no. 3 (1986): 61–67; Robert P. Shay, "Bank Credit Card Pricing: Is the Market Working?" *Journal of Retail Banking* 10, no. 1 (spring 1987): 26–32; Donald Simonson, "Relax and Enjoy the Credit Card Bonanza," *United States Banker* 102, no. 5 (May 1992): 77–78.

49. Warsh, "Credit Card Cap."

50. Seger, "Statement Before the Subcommittee," 430–37.

51. Seger, "Statement Before the Subcommittee," 430–37.

52. Charlene Sullivan, "Tax Reform: How Will It Affect Demand for Consumer Credit?" *Journal of Retail Banking* 9, no. 2 (summer 1987): 33–40. Quote is on p. 34. See also Robert P. Chamness, "A Black Cloud with a Silver Lining: The Impact of the Tax Reform Act on Consumer Credit," *ABA Bank Compliance* 8, no. 2 (winter 1987): 27–34.

53. Albert Crenshaw, "Bank Industry Says Rate Cap Would Cost Many Their Credit Cards," *Washington Post*, November 15, 1991, D1.

54. Brett D. Fromson, "Talk of Credit Card Rate Cap Shakes Market," *Washington Post*, November 16, 1991, A18; *United States Banker* 102, no. 1 (January 1992): 48; Lindsey Gruson, "D'Amato Rides a Tiger Known as Credit Cards," *New York Times*, November 19, 1991; Saul Hansell, "Bane of Banks: Those Educated Consumers," *New York Times*, June 5, 1995, A1, D2; Peter Lucas, "How to Stop Worrying About a Rate War," *Credit Card Management* 5, no. 3 (June 1992): 44–50; Krishna G.

Mantripragada and Haragopal Bannerjee, "Credit Card Interest Rate Caps Do Not Make Sense," *Review of Business* 14 (summer/fall 1992): 14; "If Rates Are Falling, Why Don't These?" *Time*, October 14, 1991, 44; David Rosenbaum, "High Credit Card Rates: A Luxurious Necessity?" *New York Times*, November 24, 1991, 2.

55. Mayo Gottliebson, letter to the editor, *New York Times*, December 6, 1991.

56. *Consumer Reports* (January 1996): 31.

57. Penny Lunt, "Do Card Ads Still Work?" *ABA Banking Journal* 84, no.10 (October 1992): 100–102; Anthony Ramirez, "MasterCard's Shift from Glamour," *New York Times*, April 9, 1990; Crenshaw, "Credit Card Firms," A1, A4; Albert Crenshaw, "Borrowing Surge Erodes Americans' Home Equity," *Washington Post*, August 25, 1991, H1, H6; Phillip D. White, "Fee Income Issues in Community Banks," *Bank Marketing* (February 1994): 60–65.

58. Michelle Singletary, "A New Breed of Debtor Shocks Credit Card Issuers," *Washington Post*, September 18, 1996, F1, F3.

59. Peter Kilborn, "Mired in Debt and Seeking a Path Out," *New York Times*, April 1, 2001, A1, A16.

60. Lucas, "How to Stop Worrying," 44–50; Albert Crenshaw, "Alarm Sounded over Growth of Credit Card Debt," *Washington Post*, December 17, 1997, C17; Albert Crenshaw, "With Credit Card Checks, Fright's in the Fine Print," *Washington Post*, February 26, 1995, H1, H9; John Meehan, "All That Plastic Is Still Fantastic for Citibank: But Formidable Competition Looms from AT&T and Prudential Credit Cards," *Business Week*, May 28, 1990, 90–92.

Chapter 4

1. *American University Eagle*, October 11, 1993.

2. John Lafayette, "Brat Pack Grows Up," *Advertising Age* 62, no. 2 (January 14, 1991), 39.

3. Visa U.S.A., Inc, "Statement Before the Subcommittee on Consumer Credit and Insurance of the Committee on Banking, Finance and Urban Affairs of the United States House of Representatives," March 10, 1994, 3.

4. Professor Robert Johnson of the Purdue University Credit Research Center, cited in Albert Crenshaw, "Crash Course in Credit," *Washington Post*, November 7, 1993, H1, H3.

5. Albert Crenshaw, "Crash Course in Credit."

6. See Kelly Andrews, "Should Credit Cards Come with Warning Labels? Marketing Maturity to College Students" (unpublished manuscript, American University Department of Anthropology, 1994). I thank Jason Fetter for gathering brochures. All citations are from credit card brochures. The Citibank mother example was cited by Ruth Susswein, Executive Director, Bankcard Holders of America, in "Testimony Before the House Subcommittee on Consumer Credit and Insurance," March 10, 1994.

7. Kaplan, "A Hot New Strategy," 46–47.

8. Duffy, "Marketing for Survival," 46–47.

9. Blayne Cutler, "Help! Dad's Doing Plastic Surgery!" *American Demographics* 13, no. 8 (August 1992): 18–20; Grace Hechinger, "Why a College Student Needs a Credit Card," *Glamour* (January 1985): 194–195.

10. Kevin Higgins, "Marketers Cultivate Youth Loyalty with Credit Card Program," *Marketing News*, November 23, 1984, 1, 17, 18.

11. Chester Swensen, "Target Lifestyles, Not Overstuffed Journals." *ABA Banking Journal* 78 (April 1986): 44, 47.

12. Cutler, "Help!"; Christine Dugas, "Credit-Card Firms Recruit New Users on Campus," *USA Today*, May 28, 1996, 1B.; Ronda Templeton, "Charge Cards Giving Students Hard Lesson," *San Antonio Express and News*, August 28, 1994, A1, A10, A18; Visa U.S.A., Inc., "Statement Before the Subcommittee," 2.

13. Vincent Alonzo, "Pennant Fever," *Incentive* 169, no. 1 (January 1995): 64–67; Terry Lefton, "Band Tour Set for Next Year," *Brandweek*, November 23, 1992; Howard Schlossberg, "College MasterValues Program Targets 13 Million 'Independents,'," *Marketing News*, March 15, 1993, 5; Jamie Schram, "How Students Choose Their Banks," *United States Banker* 10, no. 10 (October 1991): 75–78; Templeton, "Charge Cards Giving Students Hard Lesson," A1, A10.

14. Linda Punch, "Better Mark for College Cards," *Credit Card Management* 4, no. 6 (September 1991): 64–67.

15. Susswein, "Testimony Before the House Subcommittee," 1994, citing College Credit Card Corp., leading marketer of credit cards to students.

16. Gary Flood, "Oral Testimony on Behalf of MasterCard International, Inc.," testimony given before the Subcommittee on Consumer Credit and Insurance of the Committee on Banking, Finance and Urban Affairs of the United States House of Representatives, March 1994, 2, 3; Peter Lucas, "When Push Comes to Shove," *Credit Card Management* 4, no. 12 (March 1992): 30–38; Barry Meier, "Credit Cards on the Rise in High Schools," *New York Times*, September 5, 1992, A14. See also Laurie Petersen, "Risky Business: Marketers Make a Beeline for the Nation's Schools," *Adweek's Marketing Week*, May 14, 1990; Steven Manning, "Students for Sale," *The Nation*, December 27, 1999, 11–17.

17. "Credit Cards Go to High School," *Adweek's Marketing Week*, May 11, 1992, 20.

18. Visa U.S.A., Inc., "Statement Before the Subcommittee," 8.

19. Flood, "Oral Testimony," 1.

20. Arnold van Gennep, *The Rites of Passage* (Chicago: University of Chicago Press, 1960).

21. Joseph Campbell, *Hero with a Thousand Faces* (Princeton, N.J.: Princeton University Press, 1969).

22. Charles R. Babcock, "College 'Sticker Prices' Often Exaggerate Cost," *Washington Post*, October 27, 1997, A15.

23. Kenesaw Landis, *Segregation in Washington* (Chicago: Committee to End Segregation in the Nation's Capital, 1948).

24. Ken Berzof, "Rush to Refinance Student Loans Likely," *Louisville Courier-Journal*, June 8, 2002, Business 1, 3.

25. Jonathan Cohn, "Anatomy of a Murder: How Corporate Lobbyists Plotted to Kill Off Direct Student Lending," *Rolling Stone*, November 3, 1995, 41, 42, 83.

26. John Heilemann, "Debt 101," *Washington Monthly* (March 1993): 42–44.

27. Kerry Hannon, "How You're Getting Stiffed by the Student Loan Mess," *Money* (May 1992): 164–74.

28. Philip Shenon, "White House Sees a Budget Bailout in Student Loans," *New York Times*, April 22, 2002, 21.

29. Pamela Sherridan, "From Boom to Bust in the Student-Loan Business," *U.S. News & World Report*, May 22, 1989, 55.

30. Jaye Scholl, "They Never Learn," *Barrons* June 5, 1989, 26, 28.

31. The College Board, *Trends in Student Aid: 1984–1994* (New York: College Entrance Examination Board, 1994).

32. Bev Salehi, "Rising Student Debt and Higher Education Costs in a Restructured Economy" (unpublished manuscript, American University, 1997), 16; Fred Galloway and Terry Hartle, "Student Brrowing: How Much Is Too Much?" (draft prepared for the American Council on Education's Symposium on Student Debt Burden, Washington, D.C., 1994).

33. Babcock, "College Sticker Prices."

34. Albert Crenshaw, "Sallie Mae's Struggle to Save Itself," *Washington Post*, June 7, 1993, 16; Heileman, "Debt 101."

35. Dean Foust, "Student Loans Ain't Broke, Don't Fix 'Em," *Business Week*, April 5, 1993, 74.

36. Deroy Murdock, "Our Newly Nationalized Student Loan Program," *Washington Times*, December 9, 1994, A1.

37. Deroy Murdock, "Our Newly Nationalized Student Loan Program."

38. Salehi, "Rising Student Debt," 25; Jim Zook, "Record-Setting Debt," *The Chronicle of Higher Education*, April 27, 1994, A21, A24.

39. Charles R. Babcock, "Rising Tuitions Fill Loan Firm Coffers," *Washington Post*, October 28, 1997, A1, A14.

40. Mary Jordan, "Student Loan Plan Spreads Out Obligation," *Washington Post*, June 24, 1994, A1, A20.

41. *Education Daily*, August 31, 1994, 5

42. Salehi, "Rising Student Debt," 26.

43. Rene Sanchez, "Student-Loan Study Paints Bleak Picture," *Washington Post*, September 22, 1995, A12.

44. *Chronicle of Higher Education*, September 28, 1994, A35.

45. Jamie Pietras, "You Protest, You Pay," *The Nation*, November 3, 2003, 22.

46. "Aid Amendment Defeated in Senate," *Community College Times*, March 26, 1996, 8, 9.

47. Rebecca Bellville, "Higher Ed Act Reviewed by Congress," *American University Eagle*, July 7, 2003, 1, 8.

48. Ken Berzof, "Rush to Refinance Student Loans Likely," *Louisville Courier-Journal* June 8, 2002, C1,C3; David Kirp, "No-Brainer," *The Nation*, November 10, 2002, 17–20.

49. Garance Franke-Ruta, "The Indentured Generation," *Utne Reader*, (September/October 2003), 61–63; Greg Winter, "College Loans Rise, Swamping Graduates' Dreams," *New York Times*, January 28, 2003, A1, A16; Greg Winter and Jennifer Medina, "Downturn Forces Students to Seek More Financial Aid," *New York Times*, March 10, 2003, A1, A17.

50. Albert Crenshaw, "The New College Criteria: Savings Rank with SATs," *Washington Post*, December 14, 1997, H1, H4; Peter Sacks, "Class Struggle," *The Nation*, May 5, 2003, 9–34.

51. Albert Crenshaw, "Finding a Master Plan to Eliminate Credit Card Debt," *Washington Post*, October 30, 1994, H5; Heilemann, "Debt 101." See also Institute for Research on Higher Education at the University of Pennsylvania, "Graduates' Ball and Chain: Does the Burden of Debt Limit Choices?" *Change* (March/April 1995), 55–58.

52. Beth Kobliner, "Debt," *Money* (November 1995):111–14; Gene Nichol, "Educating for Privilege," *The Nation*, October 13, 2003, 22, 24; Derek Price, "Contradictions and Misdirected Priorities: The Guaranteed Student Loan Program," *Graduate Review* (1996): 98–111.

53. Catherine Lutz, *Homefront* (Boston: Beacon Press, 2002); Katha Pollitt, "Can You Spell Cannon Fodder?" *The Nation*, November 11. 2001, 9.

54. *Handbook for Military Life* (May 2003).

55. "When Credit Causes Trouble, It's Big Trouble, Report Says," *National On-Campus Report*, December 15, 2001, 4, 5.

56. Stuevern, "Just One Word," 14–20, 26–28.

Chapter 5

1. "Credit Availability in the Inner City," Joint Field Hearing before the Subcommittee on Consumer Credit and Insurance and Subcommittee on General Oversight, Investigations, and the Resolution of Failed Financial Institutions of the Committee on Banking, Finance and Urban Affairs, House of Representatives, August 10, 1993 (Washington, D.C.: Government Printing Office, 1993), 2, 35.

2. Saul Hansell, "A Surge in Second-Chance Finance," *New York Times*, March 17, 1996, Money & Business, 3, 10; Mike Hudson, "Going for the Broke," *Washington Post*, January 10, 1993, C1, C4, C6. Quote is on p. C4. See also Mike Hudson, *Merchants of Misery* (Monroe, Maine: Common Courage Press, 1996); "The Poverty Industry," *Southern Exposure* 21, no. 3 (fall 1993): 16–27; "Robbin' the Hood," *Mother Jones* (July/August 1994): 25–29; Adam Levy, "Shadow Banks," *Bloomberg* (October 1994): 7–11.

3. "They Will Gladly Take a Check," *New York Times*, December 1, 1992, D1, D2.

4. See www.paydayloan.com/newfees.html.

5. See also Peter T. Kilborn, "New Lenders with Huge Fees Thrive on Workers with Debts," *New York Times*, June 18, 1999, A1, A28.

6. Michael J. Major, "Check Cashing Services Offer New Profits," *Bank Marketing* (February 1994): 55–58.

7. Levy, "Shadow Banks"; Hudson, "Going for the Broke"; John Caskey, *Fringe Banking* (New York: Russell Sage Foundation, 1994).

8. Mark Lawrence, "Western Union Banks on the 'Unbanked,'" *Business Week*, April 5, 1993, 71.

9. Hudson, "Robbin' the Hood"; "The Poverty Industry"; N. R. Kleinfield, "Running the Little Man's Bank," *New York Times*, August 13, 1989, 37; Levy, "Shadow Banks."

10. Ken Kusmer, *Down and Out, On the Road*, (New York: Oxford University Press, 2002); Elliot Liebow, *Tally's Corner* (Boston: Little, Brown, 1967).

11. http://cobrands.hoovers.com, search "First Cash Financial Services, Inc."

12. Genevieve Buck, "More Credence Lent as Pawnshops Grow," *Chicago Tribune*, July 13, 1998, 1, 2.

13. Sarah Jay, "A Clean, Well-Lighted Place for Loans," *New York Times*, August 19, 1997, D1, D5.

14. Steve Mills, "The Pawnbroker," *Chicago Tribune*, June 11, 1995, 1, 5.

15. Krupnik quotes in Carmen McCollum, "Sometimes Viewed as Seedy Loan Brokers, Pawnshops Become an Economic Force," *Business Watch International*, July 11, 2002, online at www.businesswatch.ca.

16. Cash America, Inc., *Annual Report 1989*, quoted in Caskey, *Fringe Banking*; Hudson, "Robbin' the Hood"; Hudson, "The Poverty Industry"; Kleinfield, "Running the Little Man's Bank"; Levy, "Shadow Banks."

17. Peoples Interest Research Group, "Rent-to-Own Survey: Don't Rent to Own," 1997, online at www.ire.org/datasets/practice/vnet/CHART.HTM.

18. Peggy Jones, "Fast-Growing Companies List Appearing in Major Financial Publications," Wall-Street.com; www.prweb.comrelease/August 1999 (accessed August 8, 2003).

19. Michael Fadel, "Rent-A-Center Raises Profit Forecasts, Settles Lawsuits," www.bizjournals.com/dallas/stories, March 4, 2003.

20. See also Alix Freedman, "Peddling Dreams: A Marketing Giant Uses Its Sales Prowess to Profit on Poverty," *Wall Street Journal*, September 22, 1993; Mike Hudson, "Profiting from the Disadvantaged," *IRE Journal* (January/February 1995): 8–11; Mike Hudson, "Renter Beware," *Washington Monthly* (October 1993): 12–15.

21. Suzanne Wooley, "Plastic—For a Pretty Penny," *Business Week*, May 18, 1992, 118.

22. Linda Punch, "A New Effort to Scrub Up Secured Cards," *Credit Card Management* 4, no. 4 (July 1991): 74–77; Ray Schultz, "Hungry Marketers Chew on the Credit Starved," *Business and Society Review* 78 (summer 1991): 33–38; U.S. Information Bureau, *Credit Card Guide* (Washington, D.C.: Government Printing Office, 1991).

23. David Cay Johnston, "Block Is Ordered to Stop Advertising 'Rapid Refunds' of Taxes," *New York Times*, February 28, 2001, C1, C2; Margot Saunders, "Tax Loans Skim Hundreds of Millions from Working Poor," www.consumerlaw.org/initiatives/refund_anticipation/release.shtml; Vivian S. Toy, "City Agency Sues H & R Block Over Ads," *New York Times*, November 1, 1995, B2.

24. Fadel, "Rent-A-Center."

25. Hansell, "Surge in Second-Chance Finance," 1, 11.

26. "Credit Availability in the Inner City" (Washington, D. C.: Government Printing Office, 1993): 85–87.

27. Alex Berenson, "A Boom Built upon Sand, Gone Bust," *New York Times*, November 25, 2001, Money & Business 1, 7.

28. "Adding Injury to Injury: Credit on the Fringe," Hearing before the Subcommittee on Consumer Credit and Insurance of the Committee on Banking, Finance and Urban Affairs, House of Representatives, February 4, 1993 (Washington: D.C. Government Printing Office, 1994); Eric Bates, "Banking on Debt," *Southern Exposure* 21, no. 3 (fall 1993): 21; Annie Diggs, "They Won't Give You a Chance," Reprinted in *Southern Exposure* 21, no. 3, (Fall 1993): 22–23; Mike Hudson, "Bankers, Critics at Odds," *Roanoke Times & World News*, December 11, 1994, A1, A6, "Profiting from the Disadvantaged," 8–11; "Trail of the Tin Men," *Roanoke Times & World News*, December 10, 1994; "Ford Motors Profits Big from Financial Subsidiary," *Roanoke Times & World News*; Randy Kennedy, "Suits Say Unscrupulous Lending Is Taking Homes from the Poor," *New York Times*, January 18, 1999, A1, A15; David Lapp, "Scamming the Poor," *Multinational Monitor* (June 1991): 28–30; Sherri Lawson, "Debt in a Minority-Owned Car Business" (manuscript, American University Department of Anthropology, 1994); Eric Rorer, "Shark Bait," *San Francisco Bay Guardian*, June 22, 1994, 17–22; Paul Tosto, "Lawmakers Scrutinize Practices," *Business South Carolina*, January 15, 1995, G1, G5.

29. Michael Hudson, "The New Loan Sharks," *Dollars and Sense* (July/August 1997): 14–17.

30. Sandra Fleishman, "2nd-Quarter Foreclosure Rates Highest in 30 Years," *Washington Post*, September 14, 2002, H1, H9; Thomas Goetz, "Loan Sharks, Inc.," *Village Voice*, July 15, 1997, 33–35; Muriel Hairston-Cooper, "Leave My Mama

Alone—Predatory Lenders Target Older Women," *Washington Informer*, May 17–23, 2001, 8; Mike Hudson, "Company's Success Fires Up Wall Street," *Roanoke Times & World News*, December 11, 1994, A1, A6, A7; Kennedy, "Suits Say Unscrupulous Lending," A1, 15; Vernon Loeb, Caroline Mayer, and Ira Chinoy, "Lender Challenged on Foreclosures," *Washington Post*, May 5, 1996, A1, A20; Alan Maimon, "Household International Is Targeted by Protesters," *Louisville Courier-Journal*, May 15, 2002, C1, C6; Carolyn Mayer, Vernon Loeb, and Ira Chinoy, "High-Rate Lenders Get Low Priority," *Washington Post*, May 6, 1996, A1, A12; David Morton, "Lien Times," *Washington City Paper*, December 6, 2002, 19–34; Bobbi Murray, "Hunting the Predators," *The Nation*, July 15, 2002, 27–30; Mary Otto, "Homelessness in Region Jumps Again," *Washington Post*, May 15, 2003, B3; Michael Quint, "Profits from Higher-Rate Loans to Low-Income Home Buyers," *New York Times*, November 9, 1994; Paul Tosto, "Taking Homes from the Poor," *New York Times*, January 18, 1999, A1, A15.

31. Kim Hopper, *Reckoning with Homelessness* (Ithaca: Cornell University Press, 2003); Carol Stack, *All Our Kin* (New York: Harper and Row, 1974); Brett Williams, *Upscaling Downtown* (Ithaca: Cornell University Press 1988); "Babies and Banks," in *Race*, ed. Steven Gregory and Roger Sanjek (New Brunswick, N.J.: Rutgers University Press, 1994), 348–65.

32. Carl Bloice, "Black Youth Feel Brunt of Nation's Job Joss," *Left Margin*, July 9, 2003; Bob Herbert, "Trouble in Bush's America," *New York Times*, May 6, 2003; Andrea Hopkins, "Deeper Look at Jobs Numbers Prompts Gloom," Reuters, May 3, 2003; Jack Newfield, "How the Other Half Still Lives," *The Nation*, March 17, 2003, 11–15; Amy Waldman, "More 'Can I Help You?' Jobs Migrate from U.S. to India," *New York Times*, May 11, 2003, 4; Fred O. Williams, "Two Call Centers End Operations in Cheektowaga," *Buffalo News*, June 30, 2001, E1; www.Your_own_business@lawsuitcollection1.8m.com.

33. See also Hopper, *Reckoning*.

34. David Barstow, "A.T.M. Cards Fail to Live Up to Promises Made to the Poor," *New York Times*, August 16, 1999, A1, B6.

35. Waldman, "More 'Can I Help You?' "

36. Susan Brin Hyatt, "From Citizen to Volunteer: Neoliberal Governance and the Erasure of Poverty," in *The New Poverty Studies*, ed. Judith Goode and Jeff Maskovsky (New York: New York University Press, 2001). See also Jeff Maskovsky, "The Other War at Home," *Urban Anthropology* 30, nos. 2/3 (2001): 215–38. The full report is available at www.consumerfed.org and www.nclc.org.

37. Mimi Abramowitz, "Bad to Worse," in *These Times*, November 28, 1999, 54–56; Randy Albelda, "Farewell to Welfare, But Not to Poverty," *Dollars and Sense* (November/December 1996): 17–19; Catherine Boo, "After Welfare," *New Yorker*, April 9, 2001, 93–107; Karen Curtis, " 'Bottom-Up' Poverty and Welfare Policy Discourse: Ethnography to the Rescue?" *Urban Anthropology* 28, no. 2 (1999): 103–40; Peter Edelman, "Reforming Welfare—Take Two," *The Nation*, February 4, 2002, 16–24; Karen Houppert, "You're Not Entitled!" *The Nation*, October 25, 1999, 11–13; Karen Houppert, "For Her Own Good," *The Nation*, February 4, 2002, 20–24; Catherine Kingfisher, *Women in the American Welfare Trap* (Philadelphia: University of Pennsylvania Press, 1996); "Producing Disunity," in *The New Poverty Studies*, ed. Judith Goode and Jeff Maskovsky; Liz Kruger and John E. Seley, "The Return of Slavery: Lessons from Workfare in New York City," *Dollars and Sense* (November/December 1996): 28–31; Frances Fox Piven, "The Welfare State as Work Enforcer, *Dollars and Sense* (September/October 1999): 32–34; "Welfare Reform and the

Economic and Cultural Reconstruction of Low Wage Labor Markets," in *The New Poverty Studies*, ed. Goode and Maskovsky, 135–51; Katha Pollitt, "Shotgun Weddings," *The Nation*, February 4, 2002, 10; "Welfare Wisdom," *Dollars and Sense* (November/December 1996): 22–23. I thank Susan Hyatt for pointing out the relevance of the new Individual Development Accounts to the earlier work of Oscar Lewis.

38. Sherri Lawson Clark and John DeVault, "Is It Safe?" *Common Denominator*, May 5–18, 2003, 1, 4; Susan Brin Hyatt, "Report from the Field: The Death and Rebirth of North Central Philadelphia," *North American Dialogue* 6, no. 1 (June 2003), 12–16. See also Shari Feldman and Wendy Hathaway, "Research Report: Hope VI," *North American Dialogue* 5, no. 1 (June 2002): 13–17; Susan Greenbaum, "Report from the Field: Social Capital and Deconcentration: Theoretical and Policy Paradoxes of the Hope VI Program," *North American Dialogue* 5, no. 1 (June 2002): 9–13; Annys Shin, "Wet 'n Riled," *Washington City Paper*, March 7, 2003, 11.

39. Susan J. Popkin, "The Hope VI Program—What About the Residents?" (Washington, D.C.: Urban Institute, 2002); Debbi Wilgoren, "Housing Program Families Need Support, Studies Say," *Washington Post*, December 11, 2002, A8; "Housing Program Chalks Up Win," *Washington Post*, October 22, 2003, B1, B9; Jodi Wilgoren, "Many Face Street as Chicago Project Nears End," *New York Times*, August 7, 2003, A14; Brett Williams, "Gentrifying Water and Selling Jim Crow," *Urban Anthropology* 31, no. 1 (2002): 93–121.

40. Fox Butterfield, "Prison Rates Among Blacks Reach a Peak, Report Finds," *New York Times*, April 7, 2003; "Study Finds 2.6% Increase in U.S. Prison Population," *New York Times*, July 28, 2003, A8; Scott Shane, "Locked Up in Land of Free Inmates," *Baltimore Sun*, June 1, 2003; Gary Younge, "Thirty Percent of Black Men in US Will Go to Jail," *The Guardian*, August 19, 2003.

41. Peter Kwong, "Poverty Despite Family Ties," in *The New Poverty Studies*, ed. Goode and Maskovsky, 57–78.; Gina Perez, Nina Glick Schiller, and Georges Fouron, "I Am Not a Problem Without a Solution," in *The New Poverty Studies*, ed. Goode and Maskovsky, 321–63; Patricia Zavella, "The Tables are Turned," in *The New Poverty Studies*, ed. Goode and Maskovsky, 103–31.

42. Krissah Williams, "Home Has a D.C. Branch," *Washington Post*, July 11, 2003, E1, E4.

43. Dexter Filkins, "In Some Immigrant Enclaves, Loan Shark Is the Local Bank," *New York Times*, April 23, 2001, A1, A15; Brett Williams, "What's Debt Got to Do with It?" in *The New Poverty Studies*, ed. Goode and Maskovsky.

44. Mark Rubin, "2000 Census Numbers Reveal Higher Poverty Numbers in the District by Ward and Neighborhood Cluster," A D.C. Agenda Neighborhood Information Services Research Paper (October 2002).

45. Trudy Liederman, "Hungry in America," *The Nation*, August 18–23, 2003, 17–22. See also Loretta Schwartz-Nobel, *Growing Up Empty* (New York: Harper-Collins, 2002).

Chapter 6

1. Andrew Ross Sorkin, "Sears to Sell Card Portfolio to Citigroup for $3 Billion," *New York Times*, July 16, 2003, C1, C2. See also Dina El Boghdady, "Retailers Getting Out of Credit Card Business," Washington Post, August 26, 2003, E1, E5.

2. Bob Herbert, "Caught in the Credit Card Vise," *New York Times*, September 22, 2003, A19; David Cay Johnston, "Very Richest's Share of Income Grew Even

Bigger, Data Show," *New York Times*, June 26, 2003, 1, C2; Paul Krugman, "The Death of Horatio Alger," *The Nation*, January 5, 2004, 16, 17.

3. Frank, "Focus on the Fed," *Dollars and Sense*, 8.

4. Gar Alperovitz, "Tax the Plutocrats!" *The Nation*, January 27, 2003, 15–17.

5. Alex Berenson, "Banks Encourage Overdrafts, Reaping Profit," *New York Times*, January 22, 2003, A1, C7; Dina ElBoghdady and Douglas Hanks, "When Being Late Is Good for Business," *Washington Post*, November 11, 2002, H1, H6.

6. Albert Crenshaw, "The New College Criteria: Savings Rank with SATs," *Washington Post*, December 14, 2003, H1, H4; Stanley Fish, "Colleges Caught in a Vise," *New York Times*, September 15, 2003, A27; Grancee Franke-Ruta, "The Indentured Generation," *Utne Reader* (September/October 2003): 61–64; Thomas Geoghan, "Dems—Why Not Woo the Young?" *The Nation*, July 21/28, 2003, 10; David Kirp, "No-Brainer," *The Nation*, November 10, 2003, 17, 18, 20; Gene Nichol, "Educating for Privilege," *The Nation*, October 13, 2003, 22, 24; Adolph Reed, "Majoring in Debt," *The Progressive* (January 2004), www.progressive.org; Preston Smith and Sharon Szmyanski, "Why Political Scientists Should Support Free Public Higher Education," *PSOnline* (October 2003): 699–703, www.apsanet.org. Elizabeth Warren and Amelia Warren Tyagi, *The Two-Income Trap*. (New York: Basic Books, 2003); Greg Winter, "Rich Colleges Receiving Richest Share of U.S. Aid," *New York Times*, November 9, 2003, 1, 18.

7. Sandra Morgen and Jill Weigt, "Poor Women, Fair Work, and Welfare-to-Work That Works," in *The New Poverty Studies*, ed. Judith Goode and Jeff Maskovsky (New York: New York University Press, 2001), 152–78.

8. Robert Pollin, *Contours of Descent* (New York: Verso, 2003).

9. Glenn Canner, "The Community Reinvestment Act: A Second Progress Report," *Federal Reserve Bulletin* (November 1981): 814–23. See also Gregory Bozcar, "What to Expect When the Bank Examiners Come—and Turn Their Attention to Your CRA Record," *ABA Banking Journal* (April 1977): 35–42.

10. Chris Bohner, "The Brave New World of the Mega-Bank," *Dollars and Sense* (January/February 1996): 8–11, 40; Jonathan Brown, "Risk, Regulation and Responsibility: Reforming the Banks," *Multinational Monitor* (June 1991): 8–13; Jim Campen, "It's a Bank-Eat Bank World," *Dollars and Sense* (January/February 1999): 11–13; Jim Hightower, "Busting the Banks," *Multinational Monitor* (June 1991): 21–24; Lapp, "Scamming the Poor."

11. Kathleen Day, "Banks Promise Caution in $53 Billion Union," *Washington Post*, January 16, 2004, E1, E4.

12. See Jeff Maskovsky, "Afterword: Beyond the Privatist Consensus," in *The New Poverty Studies*, ed. Goode and Maskovsky, 470–82.

13. Dina El Boghdady, "Charging On, Cautiously," *Washington Post*, March 30, 2003, H1, H4; William Greider, "Shopping till We Drop," *The Nation*, April 10, 2000, 11–15; William Greider, "Deflation," *The Nation*, June 30, 2003, 11–14; Doug Henwood, "Not Such a Good Year, 2001," *Left Business Observer*, December 18, 2002, 4, 5; David Leonhardt, "Decade-Long Shopping Spree Is Expected to Slow in 2003," *New York Times*, December 16, 2002, C9; Katha Pollitt, "Who Needs Christmas? They Do!" *The Nation*, December 29, 2003, 9; Louis Uchitelle, "Why Americans Must Keep Spending," *New York Times*, December 1, 2003, C1, C4.

Index

Acknowledgments

I am deeply grateful to the gifts of emotional, intellectual, and material support I have received from

—my former students, now anthropologists in their own right, Marianna Blagburn, Sherri Lawson Clark, Sam Collins, and Katrina Greene, who worked with me in poor neighborhoods, where debt just kept coming up; Angie Ohler, who taught me about debt among the Nuer; Abby Thomas, who conceptualized the middle-class life course; Gina Pearson and Derek Price, who early on saw the student loan problem; Jason Fetter and Angela Guerra, who helped with student debt research; Mindy Michels, who testified to student activism; Emily Steinmetz, who helped me see some of the problems with financial aid; Heather Reisinger, who showed me the devastation wrought by the War on Drugs;

—Joan Gero, Mike Hudson, Stephen Loring, Catherine Lutz, Roger Sanjek, the late Joe Wood, and my brother Bobby, who saw the value of this project early and encouraged me along the way;

—Jeff Maskovsky, who prodded me to look beyond the local, and Susan Hyatt, who taught me about Individual Development Accounts;

—Tom Grooms, Susan Lanser, Jo Radner, and Rodger Streitmater, who helped me appreciate deadbeats; Ken Kusmer, who helped me understand the 1970s; Mieke Meurs, who pointed me to Robert Pollin; and Geoff Burkhart, who warned me about credit cards on campus;

—Maureen Hayes Fleming, who took me to the beach, gave me a clipboard, and helped me understand Madeline Smith; Peter and Linda Barton, who generously set me up in an emergency beach house later on;

—Amy Belasco, Micaela di Leonardo, Reggie Harrision, and Elizabeth Sheehan, who, in addition to their unconditional love and support, made sure I never missed a story; Yvonne Jones, who usually had a funnier story; Bruce Peck, Wendy Weiss, and John Willoughby, who tried to contain my excesses; Scott Bewley, whose anger and passion sustained my own; and Warren Belasco, who helps me think and write.

I am grateful to University of Pennsylvania Press editor Peter Agree for nurturing this effort for a very long time, and to Erica Ginsburg for her patience and good humor in guiding the manuscript through its last stages. My sons, Chris and John Henry, have lived through the years and events I describe in this book and somehow emerged as wise, funny, generous, creative, and insightful adults. My niece, Maggie, and my sister, Lucy, have understood and articulated the complexities of debt in families, and my mother, Colleen, may not have understood but has still been there to bail us out. The language of debt has no words to describe Jon Adelson's love of language, his skill at clarifying complex ideas, and his unselfishness in turning those talents to this project.

Schmitt